"I'm so grateful—both as a father a[...] new book by Arleen Spenceley. Sh[...] and writer, engaging the heart and the soul with every turn or the page. She doesn't just have a story to tell, she shares her own—with unrivaled rawness and authenticity—in a way that even the most cynical heart will be moved. I have always admired Arleen's writing, her passion, and how she gives a voice to the Lord through modern media. In *Chastity Is for Lovers*, Spenceley establishes herself not merely as a voice but, rather, the voice of and to the young Catholic Church."

Mark Hart
Executive Vice President
Life Teen

"God always allows U-turns, no matter how many mistakes we've made. But there is also a better and truly beautiful way to live one's life and avoid the pain that comes when one doesn't follow God's perfect plan for sexuality. What a powerful resource Arleen is providing for women and men in today's oversexualized culture."

Teresa Tomeo
Motivational speaker, best-selling author,
and syndicated Catholic talk show host

"With clarity and charity, and a good dose of touching story, Arleen Spenceley has opened a space to discuss authentic chastity again. She does so not with a negative, repressive, or condemning tone but with one full of joy, hope, and humor. She reminds us all to find, in every state of life, the truth that our hearts really long for: the deepest love, the one every heart is made for!"

Bill Donaghy
Curriculum specialist, international speaker, and teacher
Theology of the Body Institute

"A frank, funny, honest, and insightful look at one of the most important topics of our generation. Arleen beautifully unpacks what chastity is (and isn't!) and provides us with practical examples on how to live it in our everyday lives."

Bob Rice
Author of *A 40-Day Spiritual Workout for Catholics*

"I commend Arleen for not only writing this book, but also for taking a stand in a world that encourages non-marital sex and where chastity is mocked or disregarded by the general public. She affirms the will of God for all of us: greater intimacy with Jesus, who satisfies all our needs!"

Wilna van Beek
Motivational speaker and chastity advocate

"Arleen's courageous witness of being a virgin in the twenty-first century is awe inspiring. Every young person that reads this book will be encouraged to save sex!"

Justin Fatica
Author of *Hard as Nails* and *Win It All*

"Wise, insightful, and relatable. Arleen Spenceley brings clarity and truth to a topic that is both widely misunderstood and widely disrespected. Her words are a beautiful reminder of the sanctity, purity, and power of human sexuality."

Mandy Dobbelmann
Singer/songwriter of "Just Like Me"

"Perfectly titled, *Chastity Is for Lovers* is a book that brings light to the beautiful truth that deep, authentic love comes from living an integrated, chaste lifestyle. Arleen Spenceley uses stories, personal experience, humor, and Church teaching to express what we all know deep in our hearts—we yearn for something more than this world offers: a love story that allows living life to the full! People of all ages, states of life, and vocations can benefit from this down-to-earth, honest, and fun approach to the misunderstood virtue of chastity."

Jackie Francois Angel
Singer/songwriter of "Your Kingdom Is Glorious"

"Our culture is bombarded with sex talk, but *Chastity Is for Lovers* initiates a conversation about true vulnerability. With her trademark mix of logic, heart, and self-deprecating humor, Arleen Spenceley makes a compelling case for choosing the narrow gate."

Dalia Colón
Associate producer and cohost of *Arts Plus*, Tampa Bay, Florida

Chastity is for Lovers

Single,
Happy,
and
(Still)
a Virgin

Arleen Spenceley

AVE MARIA PRESS AVE Notre Dame, Indiana

Founded in 1865, Ave Maria Press is a ministry of the United States Province of Holy Cross.

www.avemariapress.com

Paperback: ISBN-13 978-1-59471-480-1

E-book: ISBN-13 978-1-59471-481-8

Cover image © Thinkstockphotos.com

Cover and text design by Katherine Robinson.

Printed and bound in the United States of America.

Library of Congress Cataloging-in-Publication Data

Spenceley, Arleen.

Chastity is for lovers : single, happy, and (still) a virgin / Arleen Spenceley.

pages cm

Includes bibliographical references.

ISBN 978-1-59471-480-1

1. Chastity. 2. Sex--Religious aspects--Catholic Church. I. Title.

BV4647.C5S64 2014

241'.664--dc23

2014018893

For my parents

To
Kiara!
Psalm 37:4

To
Kiara!
Psalm 31:4
♡

Contents

Contents

Foreword

I have never met Arleen Spenceley (the woman with five *e*'s in her name) in person. We met online after I linked her article "Why I'm Still a Virgin at Age 26" to a blog post. I admired her courage in "coming out" as a twenty-six-year-old virgin. Let's pause for a moment and think of how unusual this is today: "coming out" as a virgin. Only about half of a century ago, virginity (outside of marriage) was the norm and expected. Now it is the anomaly and unexpected. The tables have completely turned. What the hey happened? It was called the Sexual Revolution, and it is still with us, continuing to morph and mutate and grow more and more extreme.

And yet, it is no longer a revolution. Like many successful revolutions, the Sexual Revolution has become the accepted, authoritative, unquestioned Establishment. Arleen doesn't take up this historical sea change in *Chastity Is for Lovers*. Rather, she starts with the here and now, with her experience and today's sensibilities and practices, in order to set the record straight, defining terms and dispelling myths about her "marginal" lifestyle. (Alternate titles for this book might be *Everything You Always Wanted to Know about Chastity but Were Afraid to Ask, The Joy of Chastity*, and *Chastity and the Single Girl*.)

ix

No matter what your own beliefs and experiences are, Arleen will make you think (or rethink) about them. And you'll enjoy her descriptive, readable, light-touch writing style. Hers is a nonjudgmental approach, partly because she is the one constantly being judged, questioned, challenged, and warned about the "dangers" of living chastely! Foremost among these "dangers" is the supposedly frightening specter of being single for the rest of one's life. But Arleen knows that finding the right marriage partner and preparing for a happy marriage (no matter how much one desires it or works hard at achieving it) is never a foregone conclusion, nor solely within one's own power. She also knows that just having lots of sex before marriage doesn't guarantee eventually getting hitched, a fact to which millions of sexually active singles in their thirties and forties can attest.

The despair and desperation that some endure to find love is expressed in Lady Gaga's song "Do What You Want with My Body." This song perfectly illustrates the profound body to soul, matter to spirit, physical to spiritual split that has affected so many sexually experienced singles. Lady Gaga sings of being afraid that she will be abandoned, so she decides that she will only give her body (as if this is somehow safer!). The song raises the question: When will Lady Gaga give her whole self, "heart, mind, life," to someone if she is giving out parts of herself now?

We are one person: body and soul. Whatever we do with our body, we do with our soul, and vice versa. We can do mental gymnastics to try to separate them, but the reality is that they cannot be separated. Our culture is in deep pain from the fallout of this unnatural tearing apart of what belongs together.

St. John Paul II's Theology of the Body and *Chastity Is for Lovers* both teach us that living chastity isn't simply "waiting" or "celibacy" or "abstinence." Instead, it's proactively preparing for, or being in training for, true love and true sex. It's becoming whole persons so we have a whole person to give. It's living faithfully now so we can live faithfully later.

For many who have despaired that true love is even possible, Arleen has an answer. For those who tell Arleen that she is missing out on "getting some" now, Arleen has an answer. For those who believe that the goal of sex is only pleasure, Arleen has an answer. For those who feel that they have to compromise their beliefs or they'll never get married, Arleen has an answer.

In many respects, Arleen *is* an answer because she has chosen—and every day continues to choose—a life of chastity, which she believes is the surest path to authentic love. Arleen may be a lone "voice crying in the wilderness" of sex without love, sex without intimacy, and sex without lifelong commitment. And yet, like John the Baptist, she is right, and she is heralding the One who can give us everything we are looking for: true love, true sex, satisfaction, fulfillment, and peace.

Sister Helena Burns, F.S.P.

Introduction

I rested my head on the tall back of a black vinyl, executive-style chair and stared at a computer screen. The chair's wheels rolled audibly across the mat beneath it as I—a staff writer for the *Tampa Bay Times*—reached toward the desk in front of me to type. The e-mail, addressed to an editor named Jim, expressed my sudden reluctance to do what I already promised I would: write about sex. A week earlier, I had pitched the idea to Jim with confidence: a sex essay for the front page of the "Perspective" section of the *Times*, inspired in part by the demise of a bad relationship. The day I pitched it, how many readers we had—more than four hundred thousand on Sundays—hadn't dawned on me. When it finally did, all that had been bold in me got anxious.

I—a budding columnist, a practicing Catholic, and a virgin by choice—had a passion for putting what I believed in print. But that morning, the thought of revealing my virginity to the secular public sounded like a bad idea. I so warily considered the potential repercussions—unwanted attention, unsafe situations, and uncomfortable colleagues—that I forgot why I pitched the idea in the first place.

Days before Thanksgiving 2008, the clicks of my heels echoed as I crossed the terrazzo floor in a Tampa church's hall. I carried a press badge, a pen, and a reporter's note-book up to the woman in charge. I had come from the news-room to be a fly on the wall for a story about four church groups—one Lutheran, one Catholic, one Methodist, and one Reformed—that distributed food from a pantry to peo-ple in need, three days a week. The woman covered her faded jeans and her heather-gray sweatshirt with a hunt-er-green apron. It is through her that I met him.

He unfolded a chair for me next to his under an awning at a table on the sidewalk. He was twenty-seven and hand-ing out socks and sandwiches to homeless people. I was twenty-three and instantly smitten. I watched him work and took notes for the story. I never did write about him. I did, however, sooner or later date him. One afternoon, we sat side by side, cross-legged on a futon mattress on the floor in his apartment. We leaned against the lime-green wall behind us and talked and laughed. Then I asked the question.

"What crossed your mind the first time you saw me?"

He turned toward me, thoughtfully paused, looked into my eyes, and smiled before he spoke.

"I want a piece of her."

This ultimately did not end how he hoped it would.

Before he and I dated, having sex had never been an option for me. Frankly, it hadn't been hard for me to keep the promise I made to myself in adolescence to wait until marriage to have sex. By the time I met the guy from the food bank, I still had been neither kissed nor in love. At my high school—a private, Protestant one so small I gradu-ated in a class of fourteen students—no boys ever expressed interest. The boys I liked at church didn't like me back.

Hearing the words "I want a piece" while cross-legged on a futon mattress alarmed me. For the first time, I had stumbled, and unexpectedly so, into a world entirely unlike mine, in which "dating" and "having sex with" are synonymous, sexual inexperience is unusual, and admitting that you are a virgin is potentially humiliating. It happened, too, in a culture in which few people plan to save sex for marriage, and few of the people who make that plan actually stick to it.

Chastity and Dirty Cookies

Ninety-seven percent of men and ninety eight percent of women ages twenty-five to forty-four aren't virgins.[1] Eighty-eight percent of unmarried people ages eighteen to twenty-nine are sexually active.[2] Numbers like these upset churchgoing proponents of premarital abstinence. The statistics provoke condemnatory sermons at churches and church camps, preached without sensitivity to the sexual histories of the people in the pews. (Who says churchgoing young adults don't have as much sexual experience as "unchurched" young adults do?)

Knee-jerk judgments and analogies that compare people who are sexually experienced to cookies covered in dirt do not effectively define love, chastity, or sex, nor do they divulge the beauty of living them out as defined by the Church.[3] They also aren't motivators for behavior modification. Sermons that condemn people who haven't saved sex for marriage promote the misperception that there is an un-bridgeable gap between some people and God, who is the only true source of what all of us seek: hope and love.

Single, sexually active people don't fit a definitive mold. Some are pharmacy techs or journalists or professors or unemployed. Some are Democrats, others are Republicans, and others have no party affiliation. There are atheists and theists, Protestants and Catholics, people who use PCs and people who use Macs who, at the end of the day, share their beds even though there hasn't been a wedding. They have sex for a multitude of reasons but "because they don't love Jesus" isn't necessarily one of them. Sexually active people want exactly what sexually abstinent people want: intimacy, and a love that neither lets them down nor ever rejects them. They want healthy, happy relationships.

The essay I had pitched to the editor, ultimately about why I haven't had sex, would be an unprecedented opportunity to introduce readers to a widely underrated way of life—one that illuminates the path that leads us to what we all innately seek. But I worried that writing about my choice to be chaste would be too big a public window into my life. I had permission to present a fresh perspective of sex to at least four hundred thousand people without condemning or judging the ones who haven't lived it, and what I really wanted to do was back out. The day I e-mailed the editor, I tried.

Then I changed my mind.

The sex essay appeared in the *Times* in September 2009. I wrote a second, more popular one three years later. Writing about my choice to be chaste indeed *was* the window into my life I had worried it would be. But it was also a window for me into the lives of the readers who responded. There were elderly men who regretted hurting the women they dated as young adults, and college kids learning to navigate a world in which sexual activity was expected of them. There were parents who felt powerless against the influence of the society that surrounded their teens and tweens, and couples who were virgins at marriage (whose marriages have lasted up to seventy years). There were women and men of all ages who for myriad reasons wanted to keep talking about chastity and sex. All of them were bound to each other, though strangers, by a common tie: the desire to understand, experience, and exemplify authentic love.

Finding Love

Authentic love demands self-disclosure, complete commitment, and uninhibited exposure. It can be a scary prospect for people who have been hurt, over and over, by counterfeit versions. In the Catholic Church's treasury of wisdom, there is an answer to a broken heart's cry for healing, a feast for hungry souls. But the Church is one of the most widely untapped and wildly misunderstood resources in the world for discovering love. And there are reasons for that.

For some, what the Church actually says about love and sex has been presented by people who have misunderstood it. It is distorted on delivery. Others grasp parts of the Church's teaching but have never been given reasons to save sex for marriage other than "God says so." But there are other reasons—practical ones that are hard but good—and we exist in the kind of culture that needs them.

Regardless of how willing we are to admit it, most of us are deeply aware that what our culture calls the path to love and happiness does not make good on its promise. Maybe "everybody's doing it," but how loving and happy is everybody, really? Despite evidence that the world's road doesn't actually end where we're told it will, people walk it over and over because a viable alternative to it is sincerely inconceivable. Many people neither have been introduced to an alternative nor have learned that a sexual relationship is not supposed to be a path to self-gratification or self-fulfillment. Nobody has told them that a sexual relationship is supposed to be a path to God, who—in giving up his Son—taught us authentic love. Love looks like sacrifice and shifting the focus from self to others. It looks like learning together and working together, resolving conflicts rather than denying that they exist. Saving sex is an exercise in love, which has benefits before a wedding, after a wedding, and even if you're celibate for life.

This book is not about virginity pledges, abstinence rallies, or purity balls (which, for the record, are pretty disturbing). It's about a life of reckless abandon to a radical "homeless guy" who is both human and divine. It's about applying critical thought to social norms. It's about living lives that make sense in light of the Gospel regardless of how much sense our lives make to the people we meet. It's about acting on our needs for love and a Savior.

What the Church teaches about love, marriage, and sex equips us to love, Jesus-style; to embrace the narrow road and not just accept it; and to live as if marriage is for unity and community and not for gratification. It prepares us not to lower the bar, even if keeping it high means that we never meet somebody we could marry (or that finding that person takes longer than we would prefer). The Church's teachings dare us to live lives that contradict the kind to which our culture is conducive, and to love the people anyway whose don't. The Church digs deep, exposing truths the world obscures: love is selfless, marriage is a miracle, and sex isn't solely for pleasure.

Redeeming Sex

For some people, the chaste life can raise a daunting question—a question a friend and fellow blogger brought up once in an interview: "Do you ever worry that one day you'll wake up and discover you are forty-five, still single, and past your sexual prime?"

I don't. In order to worry about that, I would need to believe the purpose of sex is pleasure and that we all better get some while the gettin' is good. I don't believe either of those things. I believe that whether a person ever has sex isn't that important. What's more important is why a person has sex, and in what context. But because I don't worry about passing my sexual prime doesn't mean I don't worry at all. I do worry sometimes, but what I worry about is whether I write about this stuff with enough clarity. If I don't, and a couple of decades from now I'm *still* a virgin, I'd guess many people who've read what I've written will call my single life "proof" that the chaste lifestyle doesn't work. But the goal of saving sex isn't marriage. The goal of saving sex is saving sex (not putting it off, but redeeming it). Some people who save sex get married and some don't.

I do not know yet if I am one of the people who will get married or who won't. I do, however, know this: single forever or not, I am here to learn to love. How I learn—in part, for now, by *not* having sex—surprises most of the people I meet, which is funny for me, and weird. Some are captivated by my choice and others are scandalized. But my lifestyle is not a criticism of somebody else's. It's an option—something to try if an alternative to it isn't working for you.

I am surrounded by a society that is hyperaware of the implications of chastity and very interested in pointing them out to me. One implication is that my decision to save sex deters a lot of men from dating me. Another is that I won't know what to do or expect on my wedding night. Another still is that the average teenager has more sexual experience than I do (which is totally a bummer, assuming how cool I am depends on whether what I do aligns with classic adolescent behavior).

But this is not about that. This is about learning to die to self (or to die trying), and learning to be happy while I'm single and still a virgin. I am learning that the "terrible lover" is not the virgin who doesn't know what he or she is doing on his or her wedding night, and I'm learning that vocations are designed to result in the destruction of self-absorption. Finally, I'm learning that there are two kinds of sex: One is the world's version, which is primarily for pleasure. The other is sex as God designed it, which is for procreation and unity, and involves the creation of a unique, pleasurable sexual relationship. I am finding that all of us—single, married, and religious—are called to learn to love.

But there's a catch.

We live in a culture that encourages us to date for maladaptive reasons, to treat love like it's a feeling, and to seek with our whole lives what we want rather than what others need. We live in a culture that isn't conducive to love. It mocks us when we model it, says there's something wrong with us for trying, and is never, ever going to cater to us. This is why I sometimes have had to ask myself the following question: what do I know that makes me OK with that?

The answer? Everything you will read in this book.

Chapter 1 differentiates chastity from abstinence and explores its important role in every state of life.

Chapter 2 identifies virginity as an intrinsically affirming, valuable choice, describes what it's like to be virgin in our culture, and responds to our culture's response to virginity.

Chapter 3 explains why the first step to discovering your vocation is seeking the kingdom of God.

Chapter 4 explores dating—the path most people take toward marriage—and clarifies its purpose.

Chapter 5 defines love and differentiates it from being in love.

Chapter 6 covers the controversy that surrounds contraception and explains how not using contraception can lead couples toward authentic love.

Chapter 7 defines purity and differentiates it from the myths created and damage done by "purity culture."

Chapter 8, a conclusion, clarifies what it means to be human, and explains why people who practice chastity are misunderstood.

It is by the grace of God that I discovered what follows in a culture that distracts us from it. It is for his greater glory that I share it. To live out love, marriage, and sex as each was designed takes discipline and courage in our culture. So does learning to love. When we do, we won't fit in. In fact, we'll mostly stand out. May what you read make you OK with that, and may it remind you that you are not alone.

Chastity

A Better Sexual Ethic

"Only the chaste man and the chaste woman are capable of true love."

—*St. John Paul II*

Four days a week, a phone and a police scanner compete for my attention at the second desk from the left, second row, in a *Tampa Bay Times* newsroom. While I write, I answer calls from Pasco County's general public and listen to dispatchers and deputies work car crashes and domestic disputes. What I do outside the newsroom—such as be a virgin and blog about it—hardly comes up in conversation with colleagues, which, for workflow's sake, is probably for the best. But even my colleagues can't evade discussion of a topic I talk about a lot outside of work. Our culture's relationship with sex, tied today to a widespread quest for a better sexual ethic, is as popular in casual conversation as it is important.

Around three o'clock on weekday afternoons, the news staff at the Port Richey bureau of the *Times* stops working. We save story drafts, end internal calls, and congregate in the corner of the newsroom closest to the exit. Our press badges hang from the lanyards around our necks as we parade out the glass door, across the staff parking lot, into a mostly dirt yard, and through a gate in a chain-link fence. The trip ends where we are recognized as regulars and likely to loiter if we aren't on deadline: at Dunkin' Donuts.

The outing, which we call "the walk," is a nearly thirty-year-old tradition, prized by the Pasco news staff and pivotal in the cultivation of camaraderie and the restoration of blood flow to our legs. During "the walk" one afternoon, a photojournalism intern pointed at the yellow bumper sticker on the rear windshield of my car. Above the whir of the cars bound north and south on US Highway 19 to our right, he read it aloud: "Chastity Is for lovers." He tilted his head to a side, evidently perplexed. "How can chastity be for lovers if chastity means you can't have sex?"

I smiled and said, "It doesn't."

The intern's assumption reflected a popular but deficient definition of chastity—a misconception of it that persists in our culture because a lot of people use "chastity" interchangeably with words not actually synonymous with it. So, like the intern puzzled by my bumper sticker, the average adult detects no difference between "chastity" and "abstinence." The word chastity triggers thoughts of barbaric belts or perpetual virginity, of purity balls or abstinence pledges, of "an impossible standard of sexual piety unfairly exclusive to women," according to an anonymous respondent of an informal survey I conducted, or of eras long past in which innocent adolescents courted, married, and over time turned into our grandparents.

But that isn't chastity. Chastity is actually a virtue that results in authentic love, and misconceptions of it create deterrents to it. In a world that not solely condones but encourages nonmarital sex, chastity as an option is usually perceived as quaint and is quickly mocked or disregarded by the general public. "This reads like something your grandma wrote in the forties," one reader tweeted about one of my chastity-laden sex essays in the *Times*. Thoughtless dismissal of chastity fails to consider seriously the benefits of a level of sexual self-control that demands more of us than serial monogamy. Some consider "chaste sex" to be an oxymoron; others mistakenly presume chastity is expected of women but not of men. All of this produces an aversion to chastity.

When chastity is real, it is as important to practice it while you're married and sexually active as it is to practice it while you're not. It isn't for women; it's for *people*. It simultaneously requires and elicits the courage to be the people we were created to be, designed to give and receive authentic love, and to believe *all* our drives—sex or otherwise—can be within our control.

Chastity Is Not Abstinence

If I could go back to "the walk" the afternoon the intern read my bumper sticker, I would boldly and bluntly declare a clearer truth: *chastity is not abstinence.*

Abstinence, in the realm of sexuality, is refraining from having sex, but chastity is "the successful integration of sexuality within the person," according to the *Catechism of the Catholic Church* (CCC 2237). I'm neither a theologian nor articulate in catechesis, so at first I tripped over the definition. Now, it captivates me.

Integration. To integrate is to unite, to make into one what ought to be one. Integration puts the parts together that are better together. In other words, *chastity is a virtue that aims to integrate sexuality with the rest of the stuff that makes us human.*

So chastity preserves the unions between body and soul, reason and passion, fertility and pleasure. Chastity enables us to respect each other and ourselves. It upholds dignity, promotes integrity, and allows a person to experience love as God designed it. It helps heal the wounds of our pasts (whether inflicted by others or self-inflicted). Chastity neither pretends sexuality doesn't exist nor treats it as if it is the only significant part of a person. Chastity doesn't condemn the people who haven't always practiced it. It puts sexuality where sexuality best fits.

Chastity for the Newly Abstinent: An Interview with Becki Alford

"Chaste living can be difficult and often seems impossible in a culture . . . that indoctrinates us with the idea that we must have a sexual partner in order to 'be normal,'" said Becki Alford, a single mom and writer. She continued:

> One of the best remedies for someone thrust into a celibate way of life after being sexually active is meditation on the Song of Songs. . . . In this mystical poetry of erotic nature, we can begin to understand that God chose to create our desire for the opposite sex and the expression of those desires through sexual union as an icon of his desire to be in relationship with humanity as a whole, and [with] each one of us individually. . . . Take comfort in the fact that as we give up being sexually active through chaste living after divorce, separation, or conversion from a sexually active lifestyle outside marriage, we are being invited to greater intimacy with

Jesus as we offer our desires to him. Entering into this intimacy is the ultimate goal of our destiny as sons and daughters of God. . . . When the piercing fire of rejection and loneliness ensues, his consolation awaits us. . . .

Chastity "includes an apprenticeship in self-mastery" (CCC 2239), so like abstinence, it requires discipline. But unlike abstinence, it requires critical thought. People who are chaste make choices that align with their vocations and states of life, and they consider the implications of their potential actions before deciding the time is right to have sex. Chastity is for everyone: female or male; straight or LGBTQ; single, married, or religious. Like charity, chastity is patient, and kind, and forbearing (see 1 Cor 13:4–7).

Chastity never ends. Abstinence does. Chastity infuses sex with love, and love with sacrifice. Abstinence doesn't. Chastity never trivializes sex, and it refuses to use or objectify people. It says we can have what we want when what we want is good for us and it equips us to discern whether it is.

Chastity looks like the person who treats a significant other first as a brother or sister in Christ. It looks like the friar who spends his time being a true friend to a homeless couple, and like the radiant nun whose unbridled commitment to Christ fulfills her more than any earthly marriage ever could. It looks like the sexually inexperienced newlyweds who are bold enough to learn together, and like the husband and wife who, after sixty years of marriage, are still devoted to each other, even when one of them is diagnosed with dementia. Maybe chastity *is* old fashioned, but to borrow a quote from a woman I met once at a church in Tampa, "The old-fashioned way wasn't broken."

According to Bill Donaghy, curriculum specialist at the Theology of the Body Institute, chastity requires "prayer, self-knowledge, [and] clear boundaries." Outside of marriage, it requires abstinence. This is not simply because "God says so," or because sex is dirty (it isn't). It's because reserving sex for within the context of marriage preserves sex's sanctity, respects its magnitude, and aligns it with love as modeled by Christ.

While we're dating or engaged, we express attraction and love in creative ways, often in public places where we aren't going to be tempted to take off our clothes. If we aren't in relationships, or our vocations are religious (i.e., we're nuns or priests or soon to be one of these), we channel our energies into other worthwhile endeavors like serving others, creating art, or exercising.

Chastity Is for Everyone

- "I gave my soul to God. I gave my body to God. If you're totally God's, body and soul, isn't that a marriage right there?" —Sister Helena Burns, Daughters of St. Paul

- "You're dedicating yourself, instead of to a woman or family, to the needs of every soul, at least every soul Christ puts in your path." —Father Steve Dardis, Legionaries of Christ

- "Chastity protects the husband and wife so their love, and the expression of this love in the marital act, is truly other-centered." —Leah Darrow, Catholic author, speaker, and former contestant on *America's Next Top Model*

- "Living chastely [gives] single parents the space and place to heal sexual brokenness and focus on our role as a parent. Discerning how we will live out the rest of our lives in relationship to others will have to come second to preparing a safe and stable environment for children as a single parent." —Becki Alford, single mom

- "[Chastity] means the same thing for me as it does for anyone else: integrating my sexuality into the rest of myself. More specifically, it means celibacy, since there's no way for me to be morally consistent and be in a sexual relationship with a man. . . . What's harder, for me, is what my spiritual director refers to as 'emotional chastity.' There are times when I feel drawn to a man, emotionally above all, but I have to accept that the sort of emotional bond I'm looking for with him isn't actually appropriate." —Joseph Prever, blogger at *Catholic, Gay, and Feeling Fine* (SteveGershom.com)

The Start of a Chaste Relationship

In the summer of 2000, Bill Donaghy parked his "sweet Chevy Lumina," crossed Haggert Street—which was littered with broken beer bottles, dirty syringes, and used condoms—and traveled a city sidewalk. He, then a missionary, had arrived in a Philadelphia neighborhood called Kensington for a two o'clock meeting with the director of St. Francis Inn, a ministry that serves the poor and homeless. Outside St. Francis Inn's soup kitchen, a volunteer tossed a bag of trash into a dumpster. Her blue eyes caught Bill's.

He approached her and asked for directions to the director's office. She gave them. When he turned to walk to the front of St. Francis Inn, she, "as she loves to tell," ran back into the building and through the kitchen, passing all the other volunteers who might have met Bill at the front. When he walked in the front door, "there she was again."

What first drew him to her were her eyes. "They were literally glowing, engaging, full of a quiet joy," he said. "The fact that this encounter was at a soup kitchen drew me instantly into her heart. She was a servant, a lover of the Gospel, a missionary."

For their first date, Bill, then thirty-one, picked up Rebecca, then twenty-four, at a bookstore and drove her to Valley Forge, a historical, national park outside Philly, where they could walk and talk. "I was in a fog," Bill said, who then was still resolving his decision to leave seminary two years earlier and his decision to end a long-distance friendship with somebody else. "Rebecca was incredibly patient," Bill said. "She's a beautiful soul, a tender, thoughtful, attentive, and considerate person who is drawn to those in the margins and has a gift at drawing them out. She has a deep and abiding love for everyone, especially the vulnerable, and most especially babies. Her heart was always the heart of a mother, right from the start." Plus, Bill said, she loved *Little House on the Prairie*, and the bands Journey and Air Supply—which he considered a bonus.

Bill calls the three years that followed their first date and preceded their wedding a purification of their passion. "By God's grace, good advice, and good intentions, we saved sex for the sacrament of marriage," he said, "but certainly there were great struggles along the way."

This is chastity.

Chastity has as its root the cardinal virtue of temperance, which requires a person to resist acting impulsively on urges. Temperance also requires us not to do A, B, or C when we know that A, B, or C will tempt us to give in to urges to do what isn't good for us.

In sex outside of marriage, partners "promise" with the language of their bodies to give something that can't actually be given inside the sacrament of Matrimony. Some who have sex outside of marriage marry each other after all, but sometimes on the basis of physical attraction—a foundation not strong enough to sustain a couple or a family for a lifetime.

For a chaste married couple, sex is not the satisfaction of an urge but a donation of self, based on a love that is free, faithful, total, and fruitful. "The sexual embrace is the most intimate, complete, self-giving, self-surrendering act a human being can engage in," Bill said. The chaste married couple creates a pleasurable sexual relationship because they have committed to each other in marriage. The vulnerability of a sexual relationship both results in and is a result of trust. The couple is willing to communicate using words and courage, to practice and to be patient, and to exist for the benefit of the beloved.

For some people, chastity is an easy choice but hard work, and for others, it's hard to grasp at all because it has rubrics in a culture that doesn't like rules. But chastity isn't restrictive like shackles are restrictive. It's restrictive like boundaries: it doesn't hold us back but keeps what is hurtful, unhealthy, or needless out of the way. We are most free when we have healthy boundaries, not when we have none. The chaste person avoids situations in which foregoing chastity is easy. Chastity requires us not to consume media that might sexually arouse us. It requires unmarried couples to dodge "dark, horizontal situations." Chaste people don't date people who don't practice chastity, and we shouldn't wait until we are on a couch with a date in a dark apartment to tell him or her we're saving sex. (I did that once. *Awkward*.)

Chastity Is for Lovers!

How can we chastely love each other outside of marriage?

- *Just do it!* Find nonsexual ways to express love: bring chicken soup when he or she is sick, send handwritten notes, or show up ready to work on moving day (or when someone in his or her family could use your help).

- *Be explicitly honest.* Instead of waiting until you've committed to a relationship with somebody to tell him or her you're chaste, bring it up shortly after you meet. Uncomfortable? Potentially, it will be, but it's far easier to walk away *then* if the disclosure elicits a negative reaction than after you've agreed to commit. (And you won't be tempted by an emotional attachment to try to make a relationship work that frankly never could.)

- *Get to know his or her family.* Instead of sharing beds, share experiences that will help you learn about each other: lunch together with his grandparents, or movie night with her and her parents. Share your hopes and goals and opinions. Share meals you buy or prepare together. Silence your phones, drive to a lake, and walk the docks while you talk.

- *Spend time with like-minded friends.* Instead of dating people who aren't chaste because chaste people are hard to find, find out where chaste people are and go there: young-adult groups at churches, young-adult conferences and retreats, or Theology on Tap. Commit to friendships with the people you meet who are chaste. Volunteer together. Dine out. Grab coffee. See movies. Share your struggles and share your hopes.

What to Do When You Mess Up

We all make mistakes. Refer, though, to one of my favorite passages in the *Catechism*, which says that human nature has been wounded by original sin, *not* "totally corrupted" (CCC 405). Regardless of what we do, we are ever-evolving animations of the image of the Creator of the universe (coolest title ever!).

If you do fall off the chastity wagon, remember this: your value doesn't change because of a momentary lapse. You *can* start over. Chastity is about making the choice over and over, every day, to love. Go to confession or seek counseling; take a break from dating and spend more quality time with like-minded friends (and less time seeking relationship advice from friends who aren't better at chastity than you are).

Three Tips for Sexual Healing from Crystalina Evert

If you want to turn your life around, there are a couple of things I did to help me on the path to healing.

- The first is confession. Go to confession and give everything over to Jesus and truly start new. Also, go to adoration. Go and just be with Jesus, talk with him, and give him everything. All your hopes and dreams, all your brokenness and insecurities. Even if it's just once a month, spending ten or fifteen minutes with Jesus in the Eucharist will transform you.

- Pray the Rosary, and keep it with you at all times, right in your pocket. The Rosary is a powerful weapon. When you are tempted, or when you're being hard on yourself, or feeling worthless, just reach your hand in your pocket and feel the Rosary beads. Think of Our Lady and imagine yourself holding her hand. Ask her for strength and just say a Hail Mary. These are things that helped me get out of that lifestyle, that helped me to heal and become a whole person.

- Never be ashamed of asking for help, of going to counseling and talking to someone. There's no shame in becoming a whole, new creation for God. Get rid of all the baggage that holds you down and maybe even handicaps you in certain areas of your life. Never be afraid to face it, own it, heal it. God says, "Behold, I make all things new," and that is his promise.

—Crystalina Evert
Bestselling author and cofounder of "The Chastity Project"

Chastity requires us to adopt a mindset in which sex is unique to married to couples. Single people don't pout about a life without sex if we understand sex to be for married people, and if we accept that we are not married people. Despite what the media implies (and despite the opinions of some of my sex essays' readers), people do not die because they don't have sex. Sex is not vital to a person's life like food and water are. For the average unchaste American adult, it is difficult to wrap one's mind around the idea that one need not be sexually active to be happy. A case in point is an anonymous comment I got on my blog once, regarding the chaste life: "Your options, and the available pool of accomplished men . . . is severely limited. 99.9 percent of all the men will have nothing to do with you, and you know it." Whoever wrote it probably intended to insult me. But whoever wrote it is absolutely right. In fact, he or she may as well have quoted Jesus: "Enter through the narrow gate. For wide is the gate and broad is the road that leads to destruction, and many enter through it. But small is the gate and narrow the road that leads to life, and only a few find it" (Mt 7:13).

It's true: chaste daters who intend to date other chaste daters have far fewer people from whom to choose than other daters do. We have to be OK with a small pool. We have to accept that a lot of the people we meet won't date us, which is a nonissue if we really date in order to find a good spouse. If you practice chastity, somebody who doesn't practice chastity won't be a good spouse for you. What equips us to accept all this is twofold: knowledge of chastity's goal, which is love, and detachment from the need to be "normal."

Chastity Is Hard

I parked my Plymouth Neon in a dirt lot and skirted the rocks strewn atop it by taking a shortcut across a patch of grass. My flip-flops finally smacked pavement when I reached the street between the parking lot and the Louis de la Parte Florida Mental Health Institute, a complex that covers the quiet, northwest corner of the University of South Florida's Tampa campus. I traipsed across a covered courtyard, where a handful of fellow grad students in the Department of Rehabilitation and Mental Health Counseling congregated at picnic tables. I walked into the building.

Inside, the cold air eradicated all evidence of the late-afternoon heat from the mid-May sun outside. I took off my sunglasses and turned a couple of corners toward classroom 1636 for the first session of my human sexuality class. I sat at the back of the room, plugged in my laptop, and pretended not to be nervous. The professor, Dr. Dae Sheridan—a young, spirited sex therapist—interrupted my

anxiety by inviting the class to shout the names we know for
sexual activity and for the body parts we associate with sex.
"Gonads!"

I yelled it like a season-ticket holder at a sold-out sports
arena. Classmates shouted other body parts (some by their
proper names, and others less so). Some students shouted
sex positions or slang words, and we laughed so hard our
sides hurt. The ice breaker, designed to desensitize us to
words bound to come up in class that otherwise might make
us uncomfortable, was the start of what turned out to be one
of my favorite classes—even if it illuminated what I didn't
then talk much about at school: my sexual inexperience.

I was a twenty-five-year-old Catholic virgin, out of
place in a graduate-level, secular sex class at a state university. It neither looked nor felt right to carry around a
thousand-page sex instruction manual, parts of which I had
to read for class. I had never done what "everybody" does,
and worried it meant I wouldn't know what "everybody"
knows. The class, I thought, theoretically could warrant
real-time discussion of chastity with a bunch of people who
probably thought chastity was abstinence. I worried that
in fumbling for the right words to explain the difference, I
would out myself as unprepared and inarticulate.

Then, in a small-group discussion in class, a classmate
shared a secret: "I'm a late bloomer," she said. I waited with
bated breath for her to elaborate. *I, too, am a late bloomer*, I
thought. *First date at nineteen, first kiss at twenty-three, still a
virgin at twenty-five. Late bloomers for the win!* "I had my first
kiss at fifteen," she said, giggling like a seventh grader in a
rousing round of "Truth or Dare." *Fifteen?* My eager, internal
pep rally ended abruptly. *If she is a late bloomer, I am keeping
my mouth shut.* I concluded that classmates who count fifteen
as late for a first kiss are not ready for an adult to disclose
her virginity.

The truth was, I wasn't ready to disclose it in that classroom.

The sexual inexperience of an otherwise average adult jars the general public. Single sitcom characters are usually sexually active, and if they aren't, they tend to be socially awkward. Often, a TV virgin's social status is a source of comic relief—which can be true in real life, too. The disclosure of my virginity has resulted in wide eyes and dropped jaws, and sometimes in concern. I don't find it difficult not to have sex, but people think that's weird. Their responses to it imply that people who choose to practice chastity must have broken sex drives, or that they are *so* socially awkward they don't even know they're socially awkward.

When the voices that surround me say there's something wrong with somebody who chooses chastity, it's difficult not to internalize that message. If "everybody" has sex, I'm a "nobody." If nonmarital sex is "normal," I'm not—unless I decide not to let the world decide what's "normal." We who follow Christ are called to live a way of life that doesn't align with the way lived out by the world around us. We are supposed to be light in a dark world (Mt 5:16), to walk a narrow road that leads to life (Mt 7:14), to love our neighbors as ourselves (Mk 12:31), and to love our enemies, too (Lk 6:35).

Is all this normal? No. Is it countercultural and absurd in a good way? Yes. So is chastity. The world doesn't understand that kind of life. But that is not chastity's problem. That's the world's problem—the result of a resentment of virtue so deep-seated it is easier to emotionally abuse the people who embrace it than to consider it an option.

But "resentment [of chastity] arises from an erroneous and distorted sense of values," wrote Karol Wojtyla (now St. John Paul II). He continued:

It is a lack of objectivity in judgment and evaluation,
and has its origin in weakness of the will. The fact is that
attaining or realizing a higher value demands a greater
effort of will. So in order to spare ourselves the effort,
to excuse our failure to obtain this value, we minimize
its significance, deny it the respect it deserves, even see
it as in some way evil.[4]

St. John Paul II connects resentment to a cardinal sin called
sloth, which "St. Thomas defines . . . as 'a sadness arising
from the fact that the good is difficult.' This sadness, far
from denying the good, indirectly helps to keep respect for
it alive in the soul."

People don't resent chastity because it's bad to be
chaste. They resent it because chastity is good but difficult.
They resent chastity because we live in a culture that doesn't
like to admit that "hard" does not negate "good."

When the World Says "Don't," Do It Anyway

In the summer of 2007, to save money and my relationships,
I stopped at a kiosk in a Circuit City to have texting turned
off on my cell phone. The decision turned out to be one in
an ascetic series, mildly protested by friends who preferred
that our communication be mediated by computers. "Nice
knowin' ya," one of them wrote in one of the last text messages I received that summer. I went on to quit Facebook
for two and a half years, Twitter for three, and texting for
a total of six.

When what I had done came up in conversation, people tended to say one of two things: "I could never do that,"
and, "Everything in moderation."

Everything.

But I say this: what obligates us to partake in a little of
everything?

"Everything in moderation" is supposed to promote self-control, but the mantra implies that the ability to partake in something moderately is what makes partaking in it at all a good idea. The mantra also implies that to partake in something is a bad idea for us if we can't do it in moderation. But when we determine how good something is by how moderately we can participate in it, we avert an important discernment process: do I actually need this in my life at all? This is part of our culture's resistance to chastity.

An old article on CNN's *Belief Blog* says couples who marry are tying the knot far later in life than ever before. "Today," the blogger wrote, "it's not unusual to meet a Christian who is single at thirty—or forty or fifty, for that matter. So what do you tell them [about sex]? Keep waiting?"[5]

Chastity says yes. But when you hit a certain age in our culture, the norm is to have sex with the people you date. Because it is a norm, it is a widely uncritically adopted part of relationships. But norms aren't normal because they're good. They're normal because we keep them that way.

Accepting a norm as good because it's a norm excuses us from using our abilities to discern what's good for us, in the same way adhering to "everything in moderation" does. But if we *can* discern, why don't we? Why does our culture do what's normal without considering whether it's actually good? Maybe deep down, we are afraid of what we might discover—we worry that in looking critically upon sex as it stands, we might not like what we see; that if we examine an alternative to the norm, we might find in it a better sexual ethic. Maybe that's scary because we know we can't discover something better than the norm and not act on it—that if and when we do make that discovery, we will have to adopt a different way of life.

chapter 2

Virginity
Easier Done Than Said

"You ARE?"
—*My maternal grandmother, upon learning I'm a virgin*

While I dialed a number for the National Center for Health Statistics, I made eye contact with the Dwight Schrute bobblehead on my desk. I used a shoulder to hold the receiver and shuffled my stack of notes until a woman answered the call. She—a researcher—had co-conducted the study that says "about 98 percent of women and 97 percent of men" between twenty-five and forty-four years old have had sex.[6] The study implies that 2 percent of women and 3 percent of men in the same age bracket haven't. So my question for the researcher was natural:

"What have you learned about the 2 and 3 percent of adults who are virgins?"

She paused.

"We didn't gather data on adults who haven't had sex," she said when she finally spoke. "It's just so rare." Then, she laughed and added, "I don't even know what their prognosis would be."

Prognosis—as if virginity were a disease, as if the only plausible explanation for an adult's sexual inexperience is a diagnosis. To spare her the inevitably embarrassing discovery of just how in her mouth her foot was, I decided against divulging my virginity. Sometimes—as I've learned—it is easier to be a virgin than to tell somebody you are. Some people pity me for my virginity (until they learn it's by choice that I haven't had sex). Others stare at me, stunned and speechless.

It's true, I tell them. I *am* part of the 2 percent of women the National Center for Health Statistics hasn't researched (which is kind of cool or kind of insulting, depending on your perspective). I'm OK with it—with having never had sex so far and with the existence of the possibility that I never will. And I am fascinated with what I learned about virginity by disclosing my own in the newspaper.

When Virginity Gets Ugly

The day before my second sex essay appeared in the "Perspective" section of the *Tampa Bay Times*, the essay appeared online. At home that morning, I pulled up the *Times's* website on my computer to look for a link to the essay. I found it on the "Opinion" page and e-mailed it to friends, one of whom instant messaged me while she read it. We laughed over memories of the ex-boyfriend I referenced in it and monitored it for comments. At first, they only trickled in.

Then my friend refreshed the story.

"Another comment!" she instant messaged. But "brace yourself," she said. "It's both incredibly mean and incredibly hilarious."

Before I had the chance to read it, my friend instant messaged me again: "Oh, wow," she wrote. "You got a ton more! They're coming in droves!"

I refreshed the essay, too, and she was right—in only seconds, the number of comments had tripled, and the new ones were worse than the first ones.

"You're a virgin because I can't tell if you're a man or a woman," one of them said.

Most of the rest implied that I'm ugly.

The feedback stung, but I was happy to have an influx of people who'd read what I had written—and I was curious as to where the heck so many had suddenly come from. Then it dawned on me: "Maybe the story is featured now on the front page of the site."

I checked. I was right.

But "OMG," I typed in an instant message to my friend. *"They put the worst picture of me ever!"*

My friend found it, too.

"Hahaha," she typed. "Hahahaha."

Then she apologized and asked, "How did they ever acquire *that* picture?"

I laughed, too, but I also fumed. A *Times* photographer had taken the picture during a photo shoot for another story. The goal the day we took it—bizarre as this sounds—was a picture of the back of my head. So I wore no eye makeup that day and a Kelly-green polo shirt I hadn't ironed, and in the front, my hair was a flipping mess. When I turned to a side and smiled, the photographer—who may have been shorter than I am—shot a photo on a whim from the sort of angle that adds chins and frightens small children. The first time I saw it, I sent him an e-mail to ask him not to put the picture in the paper's database.

Apparently, he hadn't read it, because that morning, the picture *dominated* the front page of the *Times*'s website,

beneath "Why I'm Still a Virgin" in the site's most massive
font. I was mortified. I had written the essay in part to prove
you can be chaste *and* a normal young adult, but the picture
negated the point. I didn't look like a normal young adult. I
looked awkward, and unattractive, and, apparently, gender-
less. "Of *course* you're a virgin," readers wrote. But readers
weren't reading. They were gawking. They were mocking
me. And there was nothing I could do to stop it.

I called every *Times* editor whose phone number I had
until one of them called me back.

"You've seen me!" I said to him, close to tears. "I don't
look like that!"

While I needed the slice of humble pie I got, I got it
with what nobody ever deserves: snap judgments and jeers,
what the bullied gets from the bully. I dared to *be* a virgin,
first. Then I dared to discuss it, in a culture comfortable
with explicit discussion of illicit sex but disturbed by discussion of sexual inexperience. I had a chance to choose to sit
down and shut my mouth or to keep standing—to consider
whether sharing my unpopular opinion is worth derision
and humiliation. And you know what? It is.

It is, because virgins exist—virgins who feel as if they
are the "only one" left, who dread disclosing their virginity
to the people they date for fear of rejection, who are hurt by
the looks on the faces of the people who find out, and who
want to feel less alone. If I am mocked for telling them they
aren't alone, good. It's worth it because people also exist
who aren't virgins but who aren't having sex for now, or
anymore, who are derided about it by friends and aren't
entirely sure that not having sex is possible. If I'm single
forever but proving it possible, good. It's worth it because
the greatest cause of a virgin's discomfort with his or her
own virginity is *not* virginity. Virginity isn't the problem.
The greatest cause of a virgin's discomfort with virginity is

somebody else's aversion to it. Who can own sexual inexperience if the only people who discuss it around them call it a problem? Who can consider sexual inexperience survivable in our culture if nobody admits to surviving it?

The day the awful picture of me dominated the *Times* website with my essay, brutal comments bombarded the weekend Web editor faster than he could moderate. He took down the picture and closed the comments section, which put an end to the barrage. Then he deleted all the personal attacks.

"That was the most embarrassing hour and a half of my life," I said to my friend in an instant message when it ended. But the reaction to what I had written didn't stop. Instead, it showed up in my e-mail inbox. Some people wrote that virginity in adulthood is weird, others subtly suggested I marry their sons (which *is* weird, albeit flattering), and others—who are part of the 2 and 3 percent or were before their wedding nights—said they found comfort in what I wrote. Outside the praises from people who share my sentiments, reaction to the disclosure of my virginity ran the gamut from disbelief to disgust. This is because, outside churches (and even often in them), people can't agree on what to do with virginity.

The World Is Averse to Virginity

When I was a kid, the sitcom *Boy Meets World* monopolized my time from 8:30 to 9:00 on Friday nights. In one episode, main character Cory Matthews (Ben Savage) was in his college dorm room for a poker game. During the game, a guy nicknamed Gamblin' Dan was surprised to see Cory there. "I thought you were with your virgin support group," he said to Cory.

The joke is indicative of an attitude toward virginity generally embraced by the culture in which I've grown up, as evidenced by the responses to my essay. People *are* averse to virginity. So in 2013, I conducted an anonymous survey about attitudes toward it. One respondent wrote that encouraging virginity until marriage is OK—but only until we're in our late twenties. Another wrote that virginity at marriage is good for anybody under thirty, but after that it's "worrisome" and perhaps indicative of a person's "underlying social problems"—assumptions embraced, I'm sure, by the people who made fun of me.

Adults who are virgins indeed are portrayed by the media and perceived by the public as socially awkward, if not socially inept. Consider the TLC reality show *Virgin Diaries*. The show shadows adult virgins, whose sexual inexperience is either by choice or for lack of access to partners. The first episode of *Virgin Diaries* followed an engaged couple to the altar. Ryan and Shanna, who were thirty-one and twenty-seven years old respectively, not only had never had sex, but neither had ever been kissed, both for religious reasons. Their wedding ceremony, filmed in part for the show, ended with a kiss called "television's worst" by a TV critic.

And maybe that critic is right. But if he is right, by whose standards? If a kiss—yes, a messy one—*is* TV's worst, it is only the worst if how good a kiss looks to spectators is what matters most about it. But is how good a kiss looks really important?

I have never understood the concept of "good kissers" (or bad ones). A kiss isn't good because your partner is good at kissing. A kiss is good because the person you kiss is good, intrinsically. A kiss cannot be "bad" if you love the person you kiss. It's not about how a kiss looks, but about who you kiss, and why. What somebody else says about how you kiss is *not* important. What makes Ryan and Shanna's awkward first kiss a prediction of sexual incompetence and not a confirmation of unconditional love? Their choice not to kiss until their wedding—one consistent with but not required by chastity—*isn't* bad, because to make it they had to choose each other for reasons more substantial than "he or she is an impeccable kisser."

Unfortunately, similar, skill-based standards are also widely applied to sex. Virginity at marriage is frowned upon because, in our culture, how good we are at having sex and how effortlessly gratifying sex is for couples is considered paramount. As a result, sexual self-control is widely regarded as shortsighted or archaic or an otherwise bad idea, a notion that detractors of chastity often use to manipulate or shame the people who choose to date chastely.

On the floor in front of the TV in the living room of an ex-boyfriend's Tampa apartment, I divulged my plan to save sex for marriage (for something like the third time since we'd started dating). He pouted because my plan to save sex for marriage didn't align with his plan to have sex with me as soon as possible. He crossed his arms and said what he hoped would persuade me: "Do you really want to ruin your wedding night that way?"

I laughed. Then I pulled a notebook out of my purse, wrote down his question so I would never forget it (in case I ever wrote a book), walked out, and drove home. He didn't ask the question because he cared whether I one day would have spectacular wedding-night sex. He asked because he was a manipulator. But I'm glad he asked, because his question points a spotlight toward something we have to embrace if we are going to become comfortable with sexual self-control and, by extension, with potentially long-term sexual inexperience: Seamless wedding-night sex is not a strong indicator of a lasting marriage. Being prepared for a marriage is more important than being prepared for a wedding night. And chastity is fabulous marriage prep.

Preparing for a Life of Lovin'

People who aren't proponents of saving sex for marriage often contend that premarital sex is good marriage prep. "It takes a long time to settle into a comfortable sexual routine. . . . It should be established before you promise to spend the rest of your life with someone," wrote somebody who took one of my informal sex surveys. Others agreed:

- "A lifelong sentence of bad sex will only last so long."

- "Who wants to spend the rest of their life with someone who doesn't satisfy them? I want to know the sex I'm going to be getting is good enough to keep me loyal."

- "How do you know if your marriage will work if you don't have sex beforehand? What if you get married and that night you find out . . . he has no idea what he's doing? Nobody can expect a relationship to work if the sexual element of it does nothing for you."

- And another said it's a good idea to have premarital sex because "I will already know what to expect in the bedroom after I get married. No surprises."

However, an anonymous comment on a post on my blog challenges these thoughts: "I've been on both sides of this. (I was not a virgin when I got married, but had dated my soon-to-be husband for years, and we were chaste.) The years we spent learning how better to adjust to each other, to discipline ourselves for the sake of the other and our relationship, were a far better preparation for marriage than sex ever could have been."

While thought by many to put a person on a path toward marital bliss, premarital sex can create expectations of marriage that no marriage can meet. Foregoing engagement until we know the sex is consistently gratifying sets us up to expect that marriage will be, too. This way of thinking classifies sex as "good" or "bad" according to whether each person can intuitively elicit a pleasurable response in the other—as if what makes sex good is strictly subjective. Some respondents to my sex surveys give sex only three tries with a partner before they declare each other irrevocably incompatible. The desire for a compatible partner is natural, but the assumption that compatibility and effort are mutually exclusive is erroneous.

Perhaps in sleeping with all the people we date we learn what we like and don't in sex. But we also learn to expect what we like, and, apparently, to reject relationships with the people who can't quickly give it to us. But to what are we really committed if we are unwilling to commit to a person unless we know we are going to like the sex? Why—if we love somebody—do we think we won't? There is discomfort in sex for newlyweds who have no idea what they're doing, but that doesn't mean the sex they have isn't good. Their trust trumps how the sex looks and feels.

That premarital sex is a necessity is based on an ideology that doesn't consider questions like the one a friend of a friend once posed: "What would sex be like if there was no TV to tell us what it should be like?" What a different world this would be if people were more prepared to be good at marriage than to be good at sex. Then, maybe, our culture would value the unique bond created by discovering sex together, with one person until death, through practice and communication.

Maybe a couple *doesn't* know whether a marriage will work if they haven't had sex beforehand. But if most couples have premarital sex (and they do) and a divorce rate exists (and it does), people who have sex before marriage don't know whether their marriages will work either. Sure, sex before marriage could mean there will be no surprises in bed (at least at first). But that doesn't mean a marriage itself won't be full of surprises.

Naturally, abstaining from sex before a wedding, in and of itself, is not what prepares a person for marriage. Abstinence doesn't turn us into quality spouses. In a Salon.com column, Jessica Ciencin Henriquez wrote of her own surprise: sex on her wedding night was not what her teenage church camp promised it would be. Neither was her marriage. Six months after the wedding, "the idea of separating seemed more appealing than feigning headaches for the rest of my life." She had saved sex for after the wedding, "hoping it would ensure a successful marriage. Instead," she wrote, "it led to my divorce."[7]

I agree with what Jessica implies: sermons about premarital abstinence that did not also teach chastity likely contributed to the sour start of what would be her short-term marriage. It is a disservice to adolescents to tell them that saving sex until after the wedding necessarily causes good sex and good marriages—there are so many more factors involved than that. But I disagree with what else she implies: that virginity at marriage is a mistake.

Churches similar to the ones in which Jessica grew up long have promoted premarital abstinence by talking about a stigma associated with unwed parenthood, the perils of sexually transmitted infections, how much "better" you are for not having sex than the kids who do, and how awesome your wedding night will be if you wait. However, when a church (or a school or a parent) says, "Wear this purity ring," or, "Sign this virginity pledge," but doesn't actually discuss marriage, sex, or relationships with clarity, girls and boys grow up into women and men who really only know not to have sex. What they don't know is more important: *how to prepare for marriage.*

Maybe saving sex for marriage does result in "amazing sex," but if it does, we have to define what's actually amazing. The amazing part is not the sex. The sex will probably require a sense of humor for a while. The amazing part is what's implied by the fact that you waited to have sex—your patience, your participation in the destruction of self-absorption, your willingness to communicate, and your focus on something other than gratification. These skills are not just transferable to a marriage but are necessary for a good one—and for creating a healthy sexual relationship with a spouse.

With these skills, couples can be the mutual self-gift they promised to be to each other while they stood at the altar. If they have kids, they can model for their children the skills their children will need to be good spouses someday themselves. When we don't define "amazing," the assumption is that pleasurable sex will be intuitive and effortless beginning with the wedding night, *if* you save it for marriage. Jessica banked on that before her first marriage because she was told by her church that she could.

But what Jessica's church didn't tell her is that virginity alone, like premarital sex, is not good marriage prep. Red flags in a relationship aren't dismissible because we are sexually abstinent. We need to be aware of and act on red flags before considering marriage and to remind the young people we guide to look for them, too.

When Virginity Offends

Virginity, when discussed in the context of chastity, either strikes a chord or strikes a nerve. When I wrote about chastity for the newspaper, a lot of readers who aren't proponents of saving sex sent me angry e-mails. "In the end, you clearly made no point," one guy wrote. "Try again, please, but in the future, choose the subject of your articles with a bit more intelligence," wrote another.

I have thick skin, in part because in high school I worked as a cashier at Popeyes Chicken, where—as it turns out—a lot of mean people eat. I also have thick skin because what I write is not always well received by people who don't share my sentiments. The sex stuff, more than anything else, is a sore subject. The most important part of that is this: it strikes everyone. It demands responses. And as evidenced by some of the responses I have gotten, people pick up stuff I don't actually put down. They take my lifestyle personally.

"Talk about the voice of inexperience," one reader wrote, insulted I would write about sex without having had it first myself. "Religion and sex have nothing to do with one another," wrote another reader.

Some call virginity a concept "created by patriarchy, important in women but conveniently irrelevant in men." According to one school of thought, virginity has no medical definition and as such should be abandoned as a thing. The same school of thought says we should eliminate the word "virginity" from the vernacular because Christians traditionally fearmonger young people into keeping it and shame the people who don't. This is where the conversation gets weird, the point at which virginity doesn't just offend people outside churches. It also offends some of the people *in* them.

"Virginity is just another way that people in power talk about who's in and who's out of favor with [the Church], that we set up winners and losers in a Kingdom supposedly of equals," wrote blogger Emily Maynard in a *Prodigal Magazine* article.[8] An article in the *Atlantic*, which referenced Maynard's story, says, "Not only . . . is the purity-focused Christian message sometimes harmful; it also appears to be ineffective."[9]

What is seldom considered, though, is that discussions of virginity that have been harmful to the people who have been part of them do not necessarily make discussions of virginity a bad idea. Somebody's shame-based approach to promoting premarital virginity doesn't mean there aren't good reasons to promote it, or better ways to do so. Encouraging a virgin to maintain his or her virginity doesn't mean people who aren't virgins fall out of favor. In discussions surrounding virginity, we have to be careful to acknowledge an important truth: neither virginity nor sexual experience adds to or detracts from a person's value. Value isn't even the point.

While virginity at marriage is good, degrading the people who don't save sex is not. Nor is it good to encourage premarital virginity without considering the possibility that some of the people to whom you preach aren't virgins. To tell people who are sexually experienced that they are worth less than the people who aren't does not align with what we learned from Jesus: every soul is of infinite value.

Virginity itself—particularly when perpetual—has always been held in high esteem by the Church, not because virgins are worth more than people who are sexually experienced, but because *intentional virginity is a sacrifice*. Intentional virginity shows all of us that it is possible to "give [ourselves] to God alone with an undivided heart" (CCC 2349). It is a witness to our ultimate end: heaven, where we "are neither married nor are given in marriage" (Mt 22:30) but are parts of the Bride of Christ—giving ourselves to God alone.

According to the *Catechism of the Catholic Church*, virginity "is an unfolding of baptismal grace, a powerful sign of the supremacy of the bond with Christ" (CCC 1619). Somehow, the beauty of this sign has been obscured from both sides. We have wound up with nonbelievers who think we are crazy not to have sex while we aren't married, and believers who take virginity as a criticism of their out-of-wedlock sexual experience. Regarding the former, I don't care. Regarding the latter, it isn't—or at least it isn't supposed to be.

We need a new way to talk about the "unfolding of grace" and to be reminded again that neither the presence nor the absence of virginity influences a person's worth for better or worse. We all are of infinite value because we exist.

chapter 3

Providence

A Reason for Reckless Abandon

"Commit your way to the Lord, trust that
God will act."

—*Psalm 37:5*

On a Friday night, I pulled my reading glasses off my head,
pushed away my stack of books, and buried my face in my
hands in the middle of Starbucks.

"What are you studying?"

I looked up, with bloodshot eyes and big bags beneath
them—the results of a stuck writer's frustration and a recent
all-nighter. The question came from the good-looking guy at
the table to the right of mine. I had noticed him earlier while
in line to order my coffee and resolved, when I first saw him,
to sit as far from him as I could to avoid giving in to the urge
to talk to him. Who can socialize in good conscience when
there are impending deadlines? But by the time the barista

slid my cup across the counter, all the tables far from his
were taken.

"Actually," I said, "I'm working on a book."

He—a PhD student—was knee-deep in a take-home
final exam and more interested in taking a break.

"Can I join you for a few minutes?" he asked.

"Yes," I said, "Please do." I wasn't getting much work
done anyway.

In light of his apparent interest, I happily abandoned
the plan not to talk to him. He surrendered his table to sit
at mine, and a few minutes turned out to be a few hours.
We talked about our values and our pasts and our futures,
and laughed a lot, and I kind of sort of might have really
liked him. We ended our impromptu date a half hour before
Starbucks closed.

"I'll be here again tomorrow night," he said. "You
should come."

"Yes, please!" is what I would have said with uninhibited enthusiasm had my coffee been more than half-caf-
feinated. Instead, I said, "I'll think about it," because my
deadline loomed, and I thought it smart not to take him up
on the offer, lest I fall further "in like" and forego another
night of writing to talk with him.

But before bed that night, I already had made my decision. Indeed, I would show up at Starbucks on Saturday
night—to stay home instead, I thought, would be to forfeit
an opportunity.

I arrived at Starbucks by six, anxious to show up first
(to write until he arrived, I told myself). I scanned the shop
for signs of my new friend. When I discovered he hadn't yet
arrived, I picked the same table at which we sat the previous
night, propped my feet up on the chair across from mine,
and tried to write while I waited.

Then I ate a panini while I waited.

I made a phone call while I waited.

I drank an entire iced, grande, skinny, half-caf vanilla latte while I waited. I don't remember what the barista asked, but my answer was, "I'm struggling"—as in "struggling not to cry." I tried to write again and waited more.

He never showed. I left at eleven with the writer's block I already had, plus a sudden bout of sensitivity to how single I am. I hadn't expected the previous evening's encounter to change that in a day, but I had gotten my hopes up for another date-like night.

God, why don't the guys I like ever like me back? I struggled to understand why God wouldn't act on my desire to meet somebody whose relationship with me would be a bigger deal than a brief interlude to an otherwise not so satisfying schedule: write, eat, sleep if there's time, and repeat. When I got home that night, I cried about how hard it is to write a book and out of disappointment that the meaningful encounter from the night before had not resulted in another one.

A Happy Virgin?

I am single, and I am happy, but I am not always happy to be single.

It isn't fun to feel like a third wheel, or a fifth wheel. There are no warm and fuzzy feelings in discovering, while walking and talking with a friend and her boyfriend, that I am talking to myself because they stopped ten feet back to hug. Being around friends who have kids can be tough, too. When their kids fall asleep on you, your heart is warmed simultaneously as you are aware, and sometimes painfully so, of how much you kind of want your own. A friend's wedding is a cause for celebration . . . until you realize you are the only person in the bridal party who doesn't have a date (at which point you start wishing you had your own dang wedding to plan).

Being single is especially difficult during holiday seasons, or at theme parks, where—nearly without fail—I am sandwiched between couples in lines for rides, uncomfortably privy for upward of forty-five minutes to all the ways they can publicly display their affection. What they are is a reminder of what I'm not: taken. But I have had to learn to snap out of self-pity when it hits, because feeling sorry for yourself when you're unhappy doesn't make you happy. Changing your perspective does. When we feel unhappy, is it because we're single or is it because of what we say to ourselves about being single? "Nobody wants to be with me." "I'm clearly not attractive." "I'm going to be alone forever." First, prove it. And second, when you can't prove it (and I promise you can't), consider, is it possible to feel happy while thinking thoughts like that?

Years ago, I stumbled upon a quote on the Internet, attributed to Argentinian poet Antonio Porchia: "He who makes a paradise of his bread makes a hell of his hunger." Single people who believe they'll be happy when they're in a relationship condemn themselves to unhappy existences until they're romantically involved—which isn't even wholly within our control. What all of us *can* control, however, are our thoughts. Thankfully, I am surrounded by people who make that easy for me. I come from a family that has never pressured me to find a husband. My parents are in no rush to be grandparents, my brother in no rush to be an uncle. My own grandparents are fast to remind me: "You have time," they say. "You're young."

Not everyone I meet has it so good. Many friends report a different reality—one in which parents, siblings, colleagues, dentists, hairdressers (and a host of other meddlers) consistently remind them of their marital statuses. Even if we are comfortable with our being single at thirty, forty, or fifty, somebody else probably isn't. But is somebody's inquiry into your marital status based on his or her hope for your happiness, or on a need for his or her own? Does your mom want you to get married because you'll feel better, or does she want you to get married because *she'll* feel better?

This—others' focus on how single we are—is another opportunity to practice patience and self-control, virtues at the heart of chastity. And even if other people don't see it, we know a lack of current romantic involvement can be part of God's plan for a person's life, no matter to what vocation he or she is ultimately called.

What If I Don't Know What My Vocation Is?

"I *do* know what your vocation is," says Monsignor David Toups, president and rector of the St. Vincent de Paul Regional Seminary in Boynton Beach, Florida. "Your vocation as a baptized young man or woman is to simply be the best Christian you can be. Truly, that is *the* vocation."

Single life as a vocation gets as much respect in our culture as it does attention: not a heck of a lot. From the perspective of the average adult, it is ordinary to get married, extraordinary to become a nun or a priest, and not OK to be single and be all right with it. But sometimes, I *am* all right with it, wholly aware that if I can't transcend my snooze-button addiction, or my flair for creating clutter, or my affinity for not doing laundry until it's an emergency, I'm probably not grown-up enough to be a good spouse.

But other times, I am tired of waiting to meet somebody, waiting to love somebody, waiting to marry somebody, waiting for a PhD student to show up at Starbucks. I'm too busy to worry about any of it anyway, though, right? Maybe. Or, maybe *I'm too busy because I don't want to worry about any of it.* Maybe I don't want to do the work required to resolve the tension created by being part of a culture that says single life is temporary and being part of a Church that says it might be permanent. Maybe I don't want to confess the one thing that would eliminate my single-life-induced self-pity for good: life isn't hard because I'm single; life is hard because I'm human.

I'm Going to Be a What?

Dustin sat in the pew in front of me on an ordinary afternoon at St. Frances Xavier Cabrini Catholic Church in Spring Hill, Florida. He was a Life Teen core-team member, a young adult who helped my church's youth minister run the parish's high-school youth group. I was probably still a high-school freshman. Why he said what he said escapes me, if I ever knew at all, but what he said when he turned around that day has never left me:

"You're going to be a nun."

A *nun*? No offense to nuns, but the first thought I had in response to his prediction was, "Dear *God*, don't make me do it." I didn't want to be a nun. I wanted a boyfriend (and, specifically, I wanted my boyfriend to be a boy from school two years my senior whom I pretended not to like). I wanted a boyfriend so badly I used code words to ask for one in my prayer journal every night. I *wanted*, ignoring entirely that while God wants us to come to him for our every need, he does not always give us what we want. Out of love, he sometimes withholds even urgent "wants," for reasons we don't always understand. May never understand. Yet we trust him to give us all we truly need, no matter how much we might want something else. In this way we find peace in a world that too often confuses "need" and "want."

All of us are called to one of the following: single life, married life, or religious life. But each path is a mechanism by which we are supposed to fulfill our primary vocation, which is love. Vocations are designed to result in the destruction of self-absorption, but in our pursuit of them, our selfishness is revealed.

We are participants in a paradox: we only want to be sanctified if we can be sanctified on our own terms. We will abandon our wills in favor of God's only after we have what we want. Most of us won't acknowledge lifelong singlehood as possible and aren't interested in becoming nuns or priests. So, we refuse to consider it, the way I did in high school, or we want so very badly to be married. But do we choose marriage as a vocation because we have unique needs that have to be met by marriage, or do we use marriage to meet needs every human has—needs that realistically can (and sometimes should) be met in other ways?

The point is this: "Your heavenly Father knows that you need all these things," Jesus said. "But seek first his kingdom and his righteousness, and all these things will be added to you" (Mt 6:32–33). I think of this passage every time I meet a guy I'd like to date, and I think of it as I write this book, and every time I am on the verge of getting something I want. Whatever it is, it falls into my lap, and *I realize each time, despite how badly I want it, how wildly unprepared for it I am.* I mildly regret that I didn't have the foresight to do all along all the things that would have prepared me for it. This is because I consistently seek first all the other stuff, like the kid who waits until nine at night to start homework because video games seemed like a good way to spend six hours.

Our culture, which encourages a haphazard pursuit of gratification, is complicit in our poorly ordered priorities. But so are we. We decide the vocations we haven't considered can't meet our needs. We worry God will require us to do what we don't want to do without first opening our hearts to it. We settle on what we desire before we discern. But when we pursue what we desire before we

have adequately discerned, we are robbed of an important
process.

We aren't supposed to seek first the kingdom because
God doesn't want us to get what we want. We're supposed
to seek first the kingdom because seeking it first will refine
what we want, and because seeking first the kingdom prepares us for anything.

How Do I Discern a Vocation?

Maybe you'd like to discern your vocation but don't know
where to begin. Monsignor David Toups offers this advice:

> "I'll give you an acronym: SPF. We have to use sunscreen
> if we're not to allow the dangerous effects of the envi-
> ronment in which we live to damage us. We in Florida
> appreciate that. You would fry. The higher the SPF, the
> better. SPF: sacraments, prayer, friendship."

- Sacraments: Am I receiving the Eucharist at least weekly,
  and am I receiving Reconciliation at least quarterly, to
  make sure I'm really in union with Christ in the sacra-
  mental life?

- Prayer: Am I in daily conversation with God? We've
  really got to allow that channel to be open. Mother
  Teresa was fond of saying, "In the silence of the heart,
  God speaks." Silent prayer, prayer of the heart, is so
  important for us to discern our vocation in life.

- Friendship: Am I surrounding myself with good, healthy,
  wholesome, like-minded Catholic individuals? Whom
  am I confiding in, and whom am I sharing my heart
  with? That's where good Catholic young adult groups,
  discerning groups, and retreats come in. From there, God
  will—as we trust him to—continue to lead.

❖

God Calling: A Discernment Story

In 2002, the day after the *Princeton Review* named Indiana University the number-one party school in the country, a freshman named Jason moved from his parents' house in St. Louis to a dorm room in Briscoe Gucker, where he would help maintain the school's reputation, mostly by binge drinking and going to bars with a fake ID.

In college, "I ran away from the Church," he said, but "God had a funny way of calling me back. He pretty well destroyed the life I built." Jason's grades dropped by his sophomore year—the same year his parents nearly divorced, his fraternity was put on probation, he lost interest in school, and he was depressed. "In hindsight," he said, it "was the only way God was going to get my attention."

For the break after his sophomore year, Jason returned to his parents' house in St. Louis. He agreed that summer to attend a Steubenville youth conference as a chaperone for his church's youth group. He already had been to two previous Steubenville conferences—once as a teen and once as a chaperone. He knew, then, that after Mass on Sunday morning at the conference, the priest on stage would invite the guys who intended to discern the priesthood to stand up and step forward for prayer. What he did not expect was that he would be one of them.

"The night before, [during adoration,] I said, 'God, I don't know what the hell you're doing, but you've got my attention." After Mass on Sunday, out of the blue, "God spoke to my heart." What did he say? *I want you to be a priest.* "It made me nauseous," Jason said. "I said, 'No way, you can't be asking me to do that. How am I going to explain to seventy fraternity brothers that I'm not coming back to school because I'm going to be a priest?'"

But he moved back to his parents' house to go to community college and to discern the priesthood for a year, to meet with vocations directors, and to read and to pray. Jason volunteered that year for his church's youth group, and on a retreat, he met a young woman named Katie. Katie lived across the hall from Jason's cousin at their dorm at Saint Louis University. Katie was two years Jason's junior, part of a college core team for another parish that was part of the retreat. "We started talking after that," Jason said, "and hanging out as friends." And in the middle of a year he had dedicated to discernment of the priesthood, he fell for her.

"God, this is really confusing," he prayed. "You give me a definitive call to say yes to the priesthood, and yet here you are putting this person in my life, [whom] I'm developing feelings for." He "spent the better part of the next six months completely confused." He dated Katie regardless. While they dated, he reminded her he would apply to seminary as he had planned, that his yes to God had to come first, and he would go to seminary unless he wasn't accepted or "God comes out of the sky with a shovel, hits me over the head, and says 'Jason, don't go,'"—scenarios he thought were equally unlikely.

One of the essay questions on his seminary application asked what holds him back. "I wrote about Katie," he said— about how for the first time he had a dating relationship based on Christ. He and Katie could pray together and talk together, but he also felt "this really awesome call to the priesthood." He wished God would tell him to take one path or the other.

After he submitted his application, his feelings for Katie didn't fade, but a vocations director invited him to travel to World Youth Day in Germany with a group of seminarians, a custom he understood as indicative of his unofficial acceptance to seminary. He warned Katie: "We have to break up." But before they did, both attended another Steubenville youth conference as chaperones. The first night of the conference, they prayed together.

"She was really struggling, and I was really struggling," Jason said. "We had to say no to each other and yes to God. We said, 'If we're going to start walking the walk with the talk we've been talking, we have to say it's done.'" But after they prayed, they didn't break up. Instead, they parted ways until morning, when Jason crossed paths with Katie in a hallway on his way to the conference's men's session.

"She just walked right by me and said, 'I gave you back to God this morning,'" as she passed him. *Whoa, whoa, whoa,* he thought. *Was that a walk-by breakup?* "I tried to stop and talk to her about what she meant, but she just kept walking," Jason said. Stunned and anxious, he quietly walked toward the men's session. Before he got there, he bumped into Father Michael Butler, the vocations director for the Archdiocese of St. Louis, who had mentored Jason while he discerned the priesthood.

"Jason," the priest said, "are you still dating Katie?"

Jason didn't know how to answer.

"Well, she may have broken up with me five minutes ago," he said, "because I've told her all along we have to be done. I have to say yes to God first."

That's when the priest delivered some news to Jason: he would not be accepted to seminary after all. The monsignor in charge of admissions had sensed Jason's doubt about the priesthood in his commitment to Katie, Father Butler told Jason. But Jason worried, "I had this good relationship, *and* I had this good call." He thought a yes to Katie would be a no to God. The priest interrupted: "You're sitting on a fence. You just have to jump," he said. "Beg God. Say, 'Lord, I need a sign because I can't figure this out on my own.'"

Jason agreed and said he had planned to do that anyway, that night, during adoration at the conference.

"That's a terrible idea," Father Butler said. Adoration at the conference would be among twenty-five hundred people in an auditorium with music and lights and crying and laughing and singing. "Do you really expect to see a sign in all that chaos? Every single person in this conference is in a session [right now]," Father Butler said. "Go [to the chapel]. Be alone with the Lord. Say 'Lord, I need a sign,' because you're having trouble seeing."

On Jason's way to the chapel, he silently prayed.

"I need a sign," he said. "Please be as blunt as possible."

He arrived at the chapel, opened the door, and looked inside.

"The only person in the chapel was Katie," he said. "I slammed the door shut."

There is no way that just happened, he thought.

"OK, God," he prayed. "That was really good."

Jason opened the chapel door again and silently walked inside. He slipped into the front row and sat next to Katie, who had her face buried in her hands. He tapped her on the leg.

"We need to talk," he said.

"No," she said. "I gave you back to God."

"No," he said. "I have new information."

Jason and Katie got married in 2010.

"This is going to be one of the stories Katie and I tell for the rest of our lives," said Jason, twenty-nine, who still lives in St. Louis with Katie, twenty-eight, and their daughter, Gianna. "This is the kind of stuff they put in movies."

Even after he knew he wasn't supposed to be a priest, but to marry Katie, he wondered: "Why did God say, 'Jason, I want you to be a priest'? Couldn't he have arranged this in a way that was a whole lot less taxing?"

Sure. But "sometimes God just wants your yes," just as he wanted of Abraham, who took his son Isaac—with reckless abandon—up a mountain to be sacrificed according to God's instructions (Gn 22:1–18). As in Abraham's case, God is "not always going to make you go through with it," Jason said. "He wants to see that you're faithful."

That's the part of Jason's story at which I ask myself, *How faithful am I?*

Trust Is Not My Strong Suit

I am the clay that dares ask the modeler what he's doing (see Is 45:9). And I did, during grad school, when I discovered I could not graduate if I did not first work full-time as a counselor for a semester. Working full-time anywhere would require me to resign from my job at the *Tampa Bay Times*—a job I loved. Too close to graduation to change my mind about grad school, I reluctantly resolved to quit my job instead.

On my last day at the *Times*, in December 2012, I stayed in the newsroom into the night to tie up loose ends and clean out my desk. When my editor left, I was the only one still in the building. I took a couple of trips to my car with all I had acquired in five and a half years on staff. I walked back inside a last time, to turn off the lights and turn in my key. I stood at my desk in the dark and grieved a loss—the job I loved, the job I was good at, the job I didn't even want to quit. The night ended like a sitcom's series finale: I took a last look into the newsroom in tears and left.

The new gig had perks: more money and a fridge full of food I could eat for free. I was a counselor now, at a shelter for youth, working for a salary and for the class credit that would result in my graduation. But turnover and burnout happen fast in youth shelters, and I was burnt out before I even graduated. I decided, then, to stick it out until graduation and after that, to find a new job. And I tried. I applied for more jobs than I can count from memory but landed only two interviews (at a Catholic university and a Catholic high school, respectively). I received no offers, and the short-staffed shelter sucked the life out of me: Sometimes, I worked overnight shifts. Other times, I took phone calls at one or three or five in the morning when I wasn't at the shelter. I struggled to write this book while I worked there and struggled to understand why, despite my desperation, God had not provided.

But if God wanted me to work a job I didn't want, to write an entire book while I had no energy, to dread the sound of my alarm on workday mornings, well, then I guessed I would. While I drove to the shelter on an October morning in 2013, my cell phone rang. I rolled my eyes because I expected it would be somebody from the shelter, disrupting the commute I revered like a respite. But it wasn't work. It was Samantha, the woman who replaced me when I resigned from the *Times*, with whom I had kept in touch (and who had an eye out on my behalf for job openings at the *Times*).

"I have good news for you," she said.

A job opened? I thought.

"I just put in my two weeks' notice," she said. "And I told the editor you want your job back."

"*Shut up*," I said. "Are you serious?"

"I'm serious," she said.

I burst into tears.

That nobody hired me when I tried so hard to find a job wasn't God *not* providing. It was God *providing*. I had pouted every time I thought I would get to quit my job but couldn't, because I had no idea that what God was going to give me was way better than what I would have settled for anyway. The next day, I turned in my resignation letter to the shelter's clinical director. That night, I sat down with my bible. I found a pen in it, stuck there for who knows how long. I opened the bible to the page with the pen, which turned out to be Luke 11. This is what I read: "And I tell you, ask and you will receive; seek and you will find; and to the one who knocks, the door will be opened (Lk 11:9)."

I only could respond with "Amen." I learned that night that we can be faithful because God is. My foray into the field of counseling wasn't a waste of time but a catalyst for clarity regarding trust. I learned that we can trust him with our jobs, and with our singleness, and with our vocations. I learned that there isn't a moment in which he isn't working.

Dating

A Road to Marriage

"The real question to ask is, 'Can I put up with this person?' That sounds awful, but it's important. Does she like what I like, is he easy to talk to, is she a good friend? Of course, you have to be attracted to the person; just don't let that attraction hijack you into making stupid decisions."

—*Donald Miller, in* Father Fiction

A weekend before midterms in grad school, I woke up with a stack of books and a flat tire. Upon discovering the latter, I packed a book bag and primped for a while. *You never know,* I thought. *I could meet a guy at Goodyear.* I didn't expect I actually would.

I was saving sex and taking names, like some sort of chastity ninja: sexually inexperienced and eager to explain

why. For me, dating served the purpose of finding a guy I
could marry. I wanted a good Catholic guy and was naively
confident I could meet one anywhere. In the lobby at the
tire shop, I pretended to study, distracted by a documen-
tary about exorcisms on *National Geographic* and by the
good-looking guy who watched it. He was husky and had
dark hair and big, hazel eyes, an Italian face, and a New York
accent. When a middle-aged man walked in with clenched
fists and a fight to pick about a tire, the good-looking guy
and I stifled laughs by faking coughs and making small talk.
For the middle-aged man's grand finale, he stomped out of
the store, which is when the good-looking guy and I finally
held eye contact. We smiled knowing smiles—"you think
he's crazy, too" smiles. The shared sentiment sparked a talk
that lasted until a mechanic finished fixing my car.

"It was nice talking to you," the good-looking guy said
when I stood. "Maybe we could have coffee sometime?" I
slid my stuff into my bag and, flattered by his asking, silently
applauded his courage. I slipped him my business card.
"That's probably possible," I said, and I paid my bill. At my
behest, he didn't call until after midterms. When he did, we
discussed the Bible, our friends, and our lines of work. "I
never imagined I'd meet a good lookin' babe at Goodyear,"
he said. "I'd really like to take you out to dinner."

It took a lot not to throw a fist in the air, shout, "Offer
accepted!" and end the call to host my own personal dance
party. But I played it cool, awestruck nonetheless that for
the first time since males thought I was pretty, one of them
averted ambiguity. He did not express interest in "meeting
up," or "hanging out," or "getting together." Instead, in an
impressive fell swoop, he displayed the caliber of his interest and clarified his intentions: our dinner would be a date.
We agreed to meet the following Sunday at a tiny Italian
restaurant. While the week wore on, I bought a flattering

top to wear to dinner, prayed for my frayed nerves to get it together before the weekend, and made a potentially embarrassing discovery: I had forgotten the guy's face.

"Our encounter was really brief," I wrote in a panicked e-mail to a friend. "What if I walk up to the wrong guy?" Google unearthed no pictures of him, and no social-media profiles showed up in a search. "We're meeting at an Italian restaurant," I wrote. "Italian restaurants are crawling with husky Italian men!" Because I wasn't sure who to approach, I would need for him to approach me. So I showed up early Sunday and sat on a bench outside the restaurant, beside a chalkboard that listed the day's dinner specials. When he arrived, he knew me right away. Together, we walked inside, where we sat at a corner table, close to the wall. I wore my new top, and he wore a lot of bling. He said he was from the Bronx. He was 100 percent Italian, and I was 85 percent sure he wasn't in the mob. I ate chicken picatta, and he cracked jokes. "It's hard for me to find the time to go out, what with my wife and kids," he said.

I laughed. "Nah," I said. "I didn't find a marriage license when I looked for one." He confessed to having Googled me, too, while he sipped wine and I sipped water.

I liked him.

We hugged in the parking lot before we left and agreed to see each other again. At home, I marveled at the odds that I could be enamored by a guy who wears so much bling. I felt as if I had known him for years, and hoped so hard to hear from him. He called a couple days later. During the conversation, he asked an unanticipated question: "How do you feel about strip clubs?"

I blinked blankly and braced for rejection before I finally answered: "I'm not for 'em," I said.

"And porn?" he asked. What followed—a monologue in his defense of both—resulted in an important realization: there would be no second date.

At the time, my perspective was that the only relationship that ends well is the one that results in marriage. Since practicing chastity narrows the pool of "datable" people, it could be awhile before you date again. There is disappointment in opening your heart to someone, only to have to shut it to them later. I pouted about it because I thought he *coulda been the one, dang it!* But if the purpose of dating is to meet a man I could marry, why be so bummed over one who so obviously is not somebody with whom I could spend my life? I needed a fresh perspective: although I cut ties to the guy I met at Goodyear, my venture toward a relationship with him indeed was a success. To call a practicing Catholic's attempt to date a guy who frequents strip clubs "successful" when she breaks up with him is absurd. But it's absurd in the same way love is absurd, or sacrifice. Dating relationships don't have to result in marriage in order to be called successful. They just need to serve the right purpose. My short-lived relationship with a strip-club enthusiast did: I discovered the truth about him, and I acted on it.

When Breaking Up Is Hard to Do

Sometimes it is difficult to look at a relationship's end with such detachment. Sometimes, breaking up really is hard to do. When my very first romantic relationship ended—long before I met the guy at Goodyear—I didn't cry until the day after, while I folded laundry and fell into a state of depression. That day I dwelled on how hollow I felt, on how being dumped felt as if somebody had died. I wanted to call him. Instead, I deleted his number.

In a substance-abuse counseling class I took in grad school, I learned about withdrawal, which is what happens to a person after he or she stops using certain drugs. Withdrawals could include sweats and shakes, nausea and diarrhea, insomnia and anxiety, depression and restlessness, a rapid heart rate, hallucinations, and delirium tremens. It's awful, in other words. But the return to homeostasis (equilibrium) requires allostasis (the process by which the body achieves it). And allostasis isn't easy, which is why some people relapse before the withdrawals pass. Going back to the drug before homeostasis is achieved alleviates the discomfort of allostasis, but it doesn't give the user time to stop craving the drug.

This is not unlike what happens when some relationships end. That is not to say people are addicted to each other (although sometimes that's debatable). It is normal to grieve the loss of a relationship, even when a breakup is mutual. There might be crying and coming up with all the things you wish you'd said or hadn't. There can be emotional eating, or emotionally not-eating, and heartache. Like withdrawals, breakups can be awful.

This is in part why people break up and make up (and break up and make up again). Restarting a relationship with somebody alleviates the discomfort caused by its end. But is post breakup discomfort a sign that a relationship shouldn't have ended? Probably not. Withdrawal symptoms are not signs that walking away from a drug was a bad idea. Withdrawal symptoms are natural and necessary.

So is grief. Grief over the loss of a relationship is not necessarily a sign that walking away from it was a bad idea. When a relationship ends, give yourself time. Wait prayerfully, and ask God what he wants you to learn from the pain. Over time, you may discover that you could not have learned this particular lesson in any other way.

Why We Date Is a Big Deal

Some people date because they're bored, or for sex, or connection, or free food. Others date because of pressure from friends or family, or because they are tired of feeling alone. People date because it's nice to be desired, or because of the meaning they assign to being dated—they think, "If she falls for me, then I'm somebody," or, "If he picks me, *then* I know I'm beautiful." People date because they are attracted to each other (sometimes explicably, other times not), or because they both happened to be at Goodyear. And, yes, some of us say we date to discern who could make a good spouse. But do we really? . . . Not if we also date out of boredom or for sex or free food.

If we start relationships we hope will result in marriage for reasons that aren't conducive to finding a spouse, with people who won't even make good spouses, we use dating to meet needs it isn't supposed to meet. If we are bored, we don't need to embark on the journey to matrimony. We need a hobby. The search for a spouse is not supposed to provide us with sex. It is supposed to provide us with truth.

When I date a guy, I don't *hope* to discover differences that make us objectively incompatible. The quest for truth is not a "gotcha." But if the purpose of dating is to find a spouse, its secondary purpose is to discover the truth about one another. Why? For two reasons. First, marriage requires love, and love requires truth. Second, the only way to determine whether someone is a suitable partner is through a process of discernment, differentiating between a person who would make a good spouse and a person who wouldn't.

I discovered the truth about the guy I met at Goodyear in a date and a phone call. While he is a child of God, and as such is of infinite value, his convictions were contrary to mine. How could we ever unite in marriage if we would not

unite on our firmest held beliefs? That I discovered the truth
about him is why our short relationship was a success. Dating is designed in part for that discovery, which is necessary
in somebody's search for a spouse.

Dating for "Fun"

What if, despite the purpose of dating, we would rather date
for no specific reason? Perhaps the pluckiest among us date
"just because," or for "sex without strings," and not because
we aim to find a spouse. The *New York Times* reported in 2012
that what our culture used to call "illegitimacy" is the new
norm: "After steadily rising for five decades, the share of
children born to unmarried women has crossed a threshold:
more than half of births to American women under thirty
occur outside marriage."[10]

The story followed a handful of single moms in their
twenties who, despite hardship, are raising their children
without express commitment to or from their children's
fathers. One of the women, a twenty-seven-year-old bartender, dated a department-store clerk on and off. They
conceived a child. The bartender's boyfriend "was so depen-
dent that she had to buy his cigarettes," the article read.
"Marrying him never entered her mind. 'It was like living
with another kid,' she said."

The bartender's subconscious reverence for marriage
is fascinating. From her perspective, her boyfriend's depen-
dency deemed him unfit to be a spouse. Therefore, she
decided not to marry him. Which is fabulous—to marry
him *would* have been a bad idea. But that she dated him,
lived with him, and slept with him anyway says something:
that she understood marriage to be a big deal but didn't
understand dating to be a big deal, too.

But if it isn't a good idea to marry somebody, why is
it OK to date him or her? In truth, it isn't. In our culture,

however, dating is disconnected from purpose. Dating for no reason has stolen Matrimony's thunder: We date because we want to date or to have sex or to feel warm and fuzzy, not because it's objectively a good idea or because we are sincere in our searches for spouses.

Dating without purpose lowers the stakes, and our standards tend to plummet with them. When dating becomes an end in and of itself instead of the means to an end, we don't stop to consider carefully the implications or the potential results—such as, in the case of the woman in the story from the *New York Times*, creating a permanent connection (a child) to a man she never would have married.

"The purpose of dating is a corollary of the purpose of life. If the purpose of life is pleasure, enjoyment, and comfort, then the purpose of dating becomes a way that individuals seek to maximize enjoyment," said Erik Lenhart, O.F.M. Cap. "If, however, the real, deeper purpose of human existence is union, then dating becomes a human activity centered around authentic union of [persons]. Human beings are made in God's image, and our relationships mirror the relationships of the Trinity, whose pattern of creation is an intimate, loving, and everlasting union."

Dating chastely can help us achieve that true union of persons.

"Just" Friends?

My phone buzzed on the nightstand next to my bed on a weeknight in my midtwenties. Happy to hear from him—then the man in my life—I answered. But not feeling so well and not much in the mood to talk, I was aloof.

"I'm sorry I'm boring tonight," I said.

He paused thoughtfully. When he spoke, he said something I didn't expect: "I didn't know it was your job to entertain me."

It was then, for the first time, that I understood virtuous friendship. What the guy implied was right: the primary purpose of friendship is not merely to entertain the other person or to make him or her happy. What a person gets out of a relationship is good (or can be, at least), but if a relationship is based on something you get, on what does your relationship stand when you stop getting it?

Nothing.

But there is a friendship on which a romantic relationship might be based—one in which "the two friends are united not in self-interest but in the pursuit of a common goal: the good life, moral life that is found in virtue," Edward Sri wrote in *Men, Women and the Mystery of Love*.[11] It is a virtuous friendship, the kind of friendship on which a marriage could stand—and that kind of friendship is the best kind.

The Chaste Advantage

In a bed with a naked British guy at the Hotel Chelsea in New York, Elna Baker—then a twenty-seventy-year-old virgin—considered having sex. "As a practicing Mormon, I'm supposed to wait until marriage. . . . But not just [for] intercourse. I'm really only allowed to kiss sitting up," she wrote in an essay called "Yes, I'm a Twenty-Seven-Year-Old Virgin" in *Glamour* magazine.[12] "It's hard to pinpoint exactly when I . . . ended up, at twenty-seven, single and perilously close to losing my virginity every other week."

While Elna decided against sex at the Hotel Chelsea, what she wrote chronicled the path she took to her ultimate decision to bend the rules of abstinence, to flex her standards so she could say yes to sex, if she eventually so chose. And she did, a decision she wrote about in April 2011 in another essay for *Glamour*: "Guess What? I'm Not a Virgin Anymore!"

After Elna changed her mind about having to save sex for marriage, her "dating life actually improved," she said. "By not taking sex off the table right away, I made it past the four-week mark in relationships with several different guys."[13] Because more men were willing to date her (and to commit to longer relationships), Elna concluded that what previously had made dating difficult was virginity. Her virginity, she wrote, was "a disadvantage."[14] But if a person who has planned to save sex for marriage can conclude that virginity (or chastity, for that matter) puts a person at a disadvantage when he or she dates, he or she has missed the point of dating.

Rejection as a result of virginity or chastity is a nonissue if a person dates in order to meet somebody who will make a suitable spouse. If you are saving sex for marriage, somebody who isn't willing to do the same isn't suitable for you. Saving sex for marriage while searching for a spouse in a culture of people who mostly won't save sex for marriage means most of your relationships will end shortly after they start. According to Elna, that's the result of a disadvantage. But according to the dictionary, a disadvantage is "an unfavorable circumstance or condition that reduces the chances of success." If virginity is a disadvantage because it results in few dates and short relationships with people you could never marry anyway, at what, then, are you hoping to succeed?

That people won't date you on a long-term basis because you practice chastity does not mean chastity is a disadvantage. It means you're dating the wrong kinds of people, or that dating is the "end" for you when it is supposed to be the "means." If you are called to marriage—to a sacred union designed to result in the destruction of self-absorption—*chastity is actually an advantage*. It weeds out the people who won't be willing participants and illuminates your goal.

The Higher the Bar, the Better

In an e-mail I wrote halfway through my twenties to a friend who is a friar, I vented: "I have never actually met a single guy who is what I'm looking for. As a result, I have been willing to date guys who aren't 'it,' in hopes that they would grow on me," I wrote. "[I have wondered whether] my standards are too high [and whether the kind of guy I want even exists]. Sometimes, I wonder whether I should just be single."

I wrote the note in the wake of a relationship's end—a short one I had abandoned abruptly by phone as soon as I knew the relationship wasn't for me. I cried over it every day for a week because I couldn't believe I hurt somebody's feelings, let alone over the phone. My friends couldn't believe it, either. "Maybe you should have given him more of a chance." A small part of me—the part that wants to appease the masses—understands that. But when somebody suggests I give a guy "more of a chance" when I already know he isn't for me, the rest me of has a question: why?

What purpose would "more of a chance" have served? Is a man more respected when I date him solely because he's nice, or when I end a relationship with him because I already know I won't marry him? "More of a chance" for somebody you can't marry is less of a chance to watch God show you how faithful he is—how well he knows you, and what you need, and what you desire.

Do I get tired of waiting? Yes. I get tired of waiting to meet a guy who not only will save sex for marriage but who loves Jesus. Someone who prays, who uses words to communicate, and who does what he says he will. Someone who knows emotions are a human thing, not a woman thing, and who expresses his own. Someone who acts his age, not his shoe size; who works hard and thinks critically; and who is patient, kind, and ready—spiritually, mentally, and financially—to "leave and cleave" (see Gn 2:24). But *that* guy—the guy God will arrange for me to meet, should marriage be in the cards—is a guy I'm not going to date if I'm dating somebody else.

My friar friend replied when I sent him that e-mail: "You made two mistakes. Firstly, you blindly dated somebody; secondly, you dropped him too late." By ending the relationship, the friar explained, I spared myself potential harm. "You should be celebrating!"

My search for a suitable spouse continues. How wide the gaps of time are between encounters with men I feasibly could date is frustrating but important. This is because if a person can find somebody he or she could date quickly after a previous relationship ends, and it is not indicative of luck or rebound, it may be indicative of insubstantial standards.

A friend of mine vented once about how hard it is for her to connect with men—harder than for most of her friends. She wondered what draws more men to her friends than to her. But her experience does not suggest there is something wrong with her. It suggests that most of the men she meets can't reach the bar. When the people we meet don't meet our standards, we can wait longer to meet somebody who does, or we can shift our standards. But the higher we hold the bar, the better.

It's like this: we have unfettered access to text messages and instant messaging. We can rent movies without leaving our houses. We have access to fast gratification from fast food and the Internet, which pales in comparison to the gratification we get from our iPads, iPods, and iPhones. While we are raised with devices designed to eliminate the space between wanting and getting, we are expected to become

adults who can wait. We are expected to deliver, then, what
lots of us fundamentally cannot, because the result of a
childhood devoid of opportunities to wait is not an adult
who knows how to be patient. We know this because it's
sensible and logical, which is why how we respond to it is
disheartening: we see that kids are impatient, so we accept
that kids are impatient. Kids see us accept impatience from
them, so they accept impatience from themselves. Instead
of modeling patience for children and giving them opportunities to practice it, we lower the bar. We are complicit in
creating what we don't want. In the same way, it is easy in
our culture to be complicit in creating what we don't want
in dating.

A standard all chaste daters share—no sex until after
the wedding—is the one that results in a small pool of people in which we could meet our future mates. (*Everybody*
thinks finding a spouse is like finding a needle in a haystack,
but chaste daters usually can't find the right haystack.) I am
sure it is for sheer frustration with the search for a spouse
that a lot of men and women lower that bar the way Elna
Baker did. The lower the bar, the bigger the pool. But consider the damage it does. If we are willing to date people
who won't save sex for marriage, we become complicit in
creating conditions in which nobody will.

Men who meet my standards *do* exist. But if I want
to marry somebody who can reach a high bar, I have to be
willing to hold it up. I have to be willing to reach one, too.
I have to be able manage my time, clean my messes, and
rouse enough discipline to sometimes resist the impulse to
shop online. I have be OK with not always getting my way
or doing what I want. I have to accept that other people
sometimes will misjudge and misunderstand me, and I have
to accept that their decisions sometimes defy logic—especially but not limited to in grocery stores and in moving

vehicles. I have to deal with that. I also have to accept that although objectively, I am of infinite value, I do not live in a world that believes that, or caters to me, or is even necessarily willing to admit I exist. This is why I am better off assuming the driver who is tailgating me is tailgating me because he has to go to the bathroom really badly and not because he is trying to make me angry.

Say What You Need to Say

The same man I dated who modeled virtuous friendship ended a call another day by saying he'd call me later. He never did. It bothered me because he provided me with an expectation and then he didn't fulfill it. So I had a choice: tell him it bothered me or hope he wouldn't make it a habit. In previous relationships, I had picked the latter, probably because I didn't want to come across as picky or critical. But it always backfired because it is unreasonable to expect a need to be met when nobody knows the need exists. I need a guy to say what he means and to do what he says. So this time, I told him what he did and why it bothered me. He never did it again.

Communicate. Be boldly honest. And be explicit. A man or woman who is prepared potentially to be your spouse won't retreat because you make a reasonable request or express what you're thinking or feeling. Your honesty expedites discovery of the truth.

We have to be grown-ups. We have to hone the skills that are important to single adult life but are transferable to marriage. We have to like ourselves and we have to love ourselves. I met a twenty-something woman at a park once, who—upon discovery of my master's degree in counseling during a casual conversation—spilled her guts. She would consider going to counseling, but only if the therapist agreed not to discuss "that self-esteem crap. My esteem comes from

Jesus," she said—and Jesus does esteem us. But he tells us to love others as we love ourselves, and how can we do that if we don't actually love ourselves?

Sometimes, we resist working on ourselves, doing stuff for ourselves, and loving ourselves because we think doing so is selfish. But one of the best, most unselfish commitments we can make is to becoming the best possible versions of ourselves while we're single. We won't love others if we don't love ourselves. We can't take care of others if we can't take care of ourselves. How good you are at time management and cleaning messes might not matter to you when your obligations are four undergraduate classes and twenty hours a week at Popeyes Chicken. But it does matter now, *because* it will matter later, when you work forty hours a week and so does your spouse, and the washing machine has flooded two rooms in your house, two of your kids have chicken pox, and one of your kids is teething.

Being and selecting somebody who can reach the bar involves discerning whether what you two can do together makes sense and what you two, as a married couple, could contribute to the world. It also involves asking and answering questions. Are you sure both of you know what marriage is? (If you aren't, see CCC 1607–1658 and 2331–2391.) Is he or she responsible, stable, and honest? Does he do what he says he's going to do? Does she? Is he or she spiritually, emotionally, and financially fit to be a spouse? Do you actually like this person? Are you a better person or a worse one as a result of your relationship with him or her? Are you holier? Are you OK with it if one of your future kids grows up and turns into this person? Are you OK with it if one of them grows up and turns into you? These are all questions we have to ask when we date for the right reasons.

chapter 5

Love
The Hardest Thing
You'll Ever Have to Do

"Love cannot be reduced to an ephemeral emotion. True, it engages our affectivity, but [it does so] in order to open it to the beloved and thus to blaze a trail leading away from self-centeredness and towards another person."

—*Pope Francis, in* Lumen Fidei

In the dark on the seventh deck of a Miami-bound cruise ship, I curled into a comfy chair to the left of the stage in the Latin club. A Dominican quartet played live music. I sat alone, up late for the last night of my trip. I tipped back my glass of ice water to take a swig, and the giant white napkin I at first didn't know was stuck to the glass's bottom shone like a beacon in the night. *Smooth.*

I laughed at myself when I noticed the napkin, tore it off the tumbler's sweaty bottom, and made another, more startling discovery: the Dominican quartet's drummer probably saw it happen. He had a smile on his face, at least, and a *güiro* in his hand, while he watched me from behind his drum kit. I smiled back and nodded to the beat of the merengue he played. While we held eye contact, my heart stopped before it pumped faster, and I blushed and got butterflies. For no sensible reason, I wanted to meet him. I *had* to meet him. I also had to get some sleep, in order to be ready to debark at the port at 7:00 a.m. Already past one in the morning, I resolved to introduce myself to the drummer, but if and only if the band called it quits for the night within a song or two. And as I thought that very thought, the band's vocalist made an announcement: "This song will be our last."

I'll do it, I decided. *I'll meet the drummer.* The song ended, and the drummer waved at me when I stood from my seat. We locked eyes while I walked in his direction, and he stood up as I stood in front of him. He reached out his hand, and I shook it.

"Hi," I said. I smiled, and he smiled back. Then, I panicked. *Does he speak English? Do I look nervous?* "I don't speak Spanish!" I blurted.

My awkwardness didn't faze him. Through a thick Dominican accent, he told me he had seen me watch him play twice before on the ship, once with a man. "Your boyfriend?" he asked.

"No," I laughed. "My brother."

"Can we, uh, keep talk?" he asked in broken English. I said yes and gave him my card. But the look on his face implied that he had not asked because he wanted to get to know me after my trip. He wanted to "keep talk" *now*, at 1:30 in the morning on the ship.

I shook my head. "I have to go," I said. He took my hand slightly, drew me in lightly, and kissed my cheek. I bit my lip and whimpered a little. I backed up but didn't let go. I didn't want to. My hand in his felt right, beneath the blue lights that shined on us from above the stage. My hand stayed in his until I backed up so far it couldn't. I turned away, then, and walked purposefully toward my stateroom with a smile and a heartache. As I neared the stairs, what happened in the Latin club became clear: *love at first sight,* I thought—the kind of encounter that makes hearts throb and souls pine and people whimper upon deciding not to act on it. I so often had discussed it, with people who talk about it with longing (if they believe in it) or derision (if they don't).

In my stateroom, I rolled my eyes and rolled into bed, still smiling. *Well that was nice,* I thought. But can it sustain a relationship?

More Than a Feeling

The encounter in the Latin club is reminiscent of encounters I've had in lots of other places, including but not limited to on a flight from Newark to Tampa, in a line to buy a grouper sandwich at a music fest called Cornerstone, and in the Johnny Rockets at O'Hare. Chance encounters with attractive people can be powerful. To cross paths with a person whose gaze stirs your heart starts something. For me, it is usually trouble. He and I—whoever he might be—share a "movie" moment I expect will result ultimately in a whirlwind romance. Instead, he never calls, or it otherwise fizzles fast, or I Google his phone number and discover what he *didn't* tell me, such as his real name and that he has a wife. (That really happened.)

Attraction is necessary but insufficient for a functional relationship. Nonetheless, lots of relationships start based primarily on attraction. We are propelled by the exhilaration generated by being near, or talking to, or walking around an airport with him or her. Our bodies are reacting, and we want, quite naturally, to act on that. It feels good. But what does "it feels good" really prepare us for? I scoffed as I thought about it on the cruise ship: *I can't believe people think "love" at first sight is real love.*

But who was I to judge? I, too, had expected before that it could sustain relationships, beginning with my first real date. The date, however, was awkward and at Chili's. I was nineteen and how attracted I was to the boy didn't negate how repulsed I was by the bean that got stuck to his finger because of the gusto with which he dipped his chips in *queso*. We never spoke again.

But "love" at first sight worked on my second real date, or so I thought. I was twenty and my heart pounded while I stood behind him in the queue at a Burger King. He sat across from me in a booth, where I fell head over feet and he ate fries. The date—a short stop on his road trip from his home in Atlanta to Florida's west coast to play with his Christian band—was a welcomed real-life encounter in an otherwise long-distance relationship. We initially met on MySpace, where in a private message I boldly declared that by virtue of his joining one of my favorite bands, he and I had to be friends. He, a Protestant pastor's son, had big, blue eyes, a bass guitar, and—rather quickly—a thing for me.

He wore black eyeliner, black nail polish, and black clothes. He called me "Love" and held my hand, burnt me mix discs, and wrote me poetry. From dark corners of church halls, I watched him sign T-shirts with Sharpies and pose for photos with fans after the band played. I fought the urge to glare at the girls who surrounded him after his shows and usually lost, impelled by pangs of jealousy. But when the crowd cleared and the gear was packed, he always came back for me, and we'd walk out together, arm in arm.

When the Florida-based band had no shows scheduled in the state, five hundred miles of interstate highway separated us desperately. Absence, according to the idiom, makes the heart grow fonder, but that payoff wasn't worth the ache. So with computers and cell phones we eliminated all the space between us. Tethered by technology, we constantly exchanged text messages, in bedrooms or bathrooms or from behind the counter at the fast-food restaurant where I worked. At bedtime, we put our cell phones on our pillows, so when we texted each other in the middle of the night our phones buzzed close enough to our faces to wake us. I carried our perpetual electronic conversation with me everywhere and let it interrupt every part of my life.

One night, I rode shotgun in a friend's car, out for face-to-face fun. While she drove us to wherever we were headed, I gushed about him. "He's the first thing I think of when I wake up in the morning and the last thing on my mind before I fall asleep at night," I said. "He said he wants to keep me forever."

Forever. I took a breath to marvel for a minute while I looked out the window at the black sky. He had held *my* hand and put his hands on *my* hips and hugged *me* for a half hour in a parking lot at Busch Gardens. I smiled and silently pined. What I felt I had never felt before.

At a stop sign, my friend explained what it meant. "You're in love," she said.

I'm in love. I nodded but avoided eye contact, lest it give away what I really wanted to say: "I don't believe that."

I have no idea how I would have defined love at twenty, but the thought that I was in it with the rock star didn't sit well. I *liked* him, yes—a lot. My attachment to him gained strength every time his bright eyes stared into mine, or he grabbed my hand in a public place or understood my sense of humor. I felt wanted, and I wanted to feel that for good, for the relationship to flourish into whatever would result in more warm-and-fuzzy feelings.

But love? Was she serious? I didn't *mind* a 2:53 a.m. text that said, "You're my favorite," but I hardly slept. I didn't want to kiss him, because I didn't know how to kiss and because he smoked, and I hated that. And I hated that he hadn't told his parents about us, that he hadn't awarded me first place in his "top eight" on MySpace. I hated that his ex-girlfriend still had that spot. I hated driving home in tears after long good-byes, dying just to smell a cigarette or sour-apple Big League Chew because both reminded me of him.

"Being In Love" Versus "Loving"

When we fall in love with someone, we "swoon," regardless of whether being in a relationship with him or her is actually a good idea. To be in love is sometimes to be so attached that separation is legitimately difficult. It starts with hearts that skip beats and palms that sweat and butterflies in stomachs. You don't expect it, but stumble into it clumsily. It isn't necessarily a bad thing for a relationship to start because "sparks" are what interests one person in another—but sparks have been misunderstood as perpetually necessary, as if a relationship that evolves into something different from what it was at its start is a relationship that has dissolved. But love doesn't keep the peace; peace-keeping means we maintain what we have. Love makes peace, and peace-making means we work to achieve something better. What happens to single adults who haven't been taught the important distinction between being in love and loving somebody—between peace-keeping and peace-making? We start relationships because of sparks, but with the expectation that the sparks are love, that the sparks are supposed to sustain a marriage. This is a problem, because to fall *in* love is effortless, and to *love* is the hardest thing you'll ever have to do.

According to St. John Paul II, love isn't a feeling or a sensual experience—it's a virtue that starts with friendship. In *Men, Women and the Mystery of Love,* Edward Sri writes that there are three kinds of friendship, as defined by Aristotle. The first is friendship of utility, which has as its foundation the "benefit or use the friends derive from the relationship." The second is pleasant friendship, which is based on the "pleasure one gets out of the relationship." The third is virtuous friendship, which is "friendship in the fullest sense. It can be called *virtuous friendship* because the two friends are united not in self-interest but in the pursuit of a common goal: the good life, moral life that is found in virtue."[15]

Love, according to St. John Paul II, is "produced in the will"—it's "an authentic commitment of the free will of one person (the subject), resulting from the truth about another person (the object)."[16] According to St. Paul, love is patient, kind, and not jealous; it doesn't brag and isn't arrogant, doesn't act out or react unreasonably, and doesn't seek first its own will or keep a record of somebody else's wrongs. Love rejoices in truth and "bears all things, believes all things, endures all things" (1 Cor 13:4–7).

It is not, I repeat, *not* mature love that inspired my decision to sleep with a cell phone. It was a subjective and spontaneous longing, both emotional and physical, a "warm and fuzzy" sensation that had far more connection to sentiment than to love. In fact, "no matter how intensely we experience these sensations, it is not necessarily love, but simply 'a psychological situation.' In other words, on its own, the subjective aspect of love is no more than a pleasurable experience happening inside of me."[17]

Immature love looks inward. The immature lover is "absorbed in his own feelings. Here, the subjective aspect of love reigns supreme. He measures his love by the sensual and emotional reactions he experiences in the relationship."[18] Subjective, immature love propels a person into a relationship because of feelings. It's the experience most of us would call "falling in love," a phrase that implies you can fall out of love, which means that sort of love isn't necessarily lasting.

Objective, mature love, on the other hand, compels a person to remain committed to the beloved when there are feelings and when there aren't. Objective love is what exists between you and somebody else in reality, not as filtered by lenses that are clouded by sudden, spontaneous sensations. It is based on a virtuous friendship, the pursuit of a common good, seeking what's best for your beloved, self-giving, and commitment to the other person.[19]

Mature love looks outward in two ways. First, it isn't based on feelings but on the truth about the other person, on commitment to that person as a result of the truth, and on selflessness. Second, the mature lover "actively seeks what is best for the beloved. The person with a mature love is not focused primarily on what feelings and desires may be stirring inside him. Rather, he is focused on his responsibility to care for his beloved's good. He actively seeks what is good for her, not just his own pleasure, enjoyment, and selfish pursuits." And the "emotions still play an important part, but they are grounded in the truth of the other person as he or she really is (not my idealization of that person)."[20]

This sounds nothing like the relationship I had with the rock star. I did not always agree to meet him at the Burger King off the interstate because I wanted what was best for him. While Burger King *was* a far easier stop for him than my house, which was thirty miles west of the interstate, I

met him there because it meant I could have a "fix" of time
with him earlier during his trips to Florida than I otherwise
would. It was not the result of a commitment to him that
I agreed to be part of extra-long hugs with him in parking
lots. It was the result of how good I feel when I'm in the
arms of somebody to whom I'm attracted. What brought
us together was transient, and absolutely amazing—until
our relationship ended.

When "Love" Ends

On New Year's Day in 2006, while I shopped with my mom,
my cell phone buzzed. I rummaged through my purse to
retrieve it—one new text, from the rock star, who I hadn't
heard from in days.

"Hey you," it said. "We should just be friends."

"Fine by me," I said to my mom and kept shopping.
But I *wasn't* fine. The next day I wept inconsolably for hours.
I wanted an explanation. I wanted to group hug the J. Geils
Band in thanksgiving for the song "Love Stinks" because I
hadn't heard words truer than its chorus.

But love—real love—doesn't stink. What stinks is
the pain caused by a culture that calls attraction "love." In
a famous scene from *The Godfather, Part II*, Kay Corleone
struggles not to cry while she makes a confession to her
husband, Michael: "At this moment," she said, "I feel no
love for you at all." The poignant line points to the problem
that pervades our lives when we aren't taught the difference
between being in love and loving.

Most of us won't fall in love with mobsters. Most will
fall in love with "regular" people—firefighters or financial
planners or teachers or graphic artists. We'll date them and
marry them because we fell in love with them. But in many
marriages, one spouse is eventually broadsided by the other's revelation: "I don't love you anymore."

It happened to a woman I know, whose husband of more than a decade took her out to lunch to tell her. It happened to a friend, whose husband insisted he had to leave because she deserved better. The person who professes love lost is likely to sound like a victim, as if love is so elusive that it spontaneously slipped out of his or her grip. To stop loving, by these standards, is fortuitous—an unfortunate and unanticipated turn of events beyond the control of the person who bears the news. But love, by these standards, isn't love—it is subjective, and immature, and it neglects an important truth: *you are in control of whether your love for somebody ends.*

Love Never Fails

Since their civil wedding in 1994, Richard had been unfaithful to his wife, Sheila, in a series of one-night stands and a two-year extramarital relationship. And Sheila knew it. But she didn't leave, and she didn't ask him to leave, either. Instead, she prayed.

It was frankly his fear of hell that led Richard to put an end to the infidelity in 2006. He and Sheila had their marriage validated by the Church in 2007. But it wasn't until a Saturday in Lent in 2011 that the couple had what they call their "big breakthrough." Richard sat with a priest in front of the altar at his church for confession. He didn't mention the infidelity because he already had confessed it. But during confession, something happened.

"I realized how much I deceived [Sheila], humiliated her, how evil it was," Richard said. As he left confession, "I just wanted to thank my wife for praying for me and for sticking with me." He felt as if a blindfold had been taken off his eyes, he said. He suddenly was deeply aware of her sacrifice, of the "heavy burden she carried for our marriage and our children." That night, he invited her out for a date.

"I was nervous," Sheila said, because a date night was entirely out of the ordinary—they hadn't had one, in fact, since before their four children were born. Over dinner at a Mexican restaurant, Richard spilled his guts.

"I remember sincerely apologizing to her for the first time," he said. Sheila cried, she said, and despite the pain her husband had put her through, accepted his apology. "Christ sacrificed his whole life for us. Why wouldn't I go through everything I got through? What makes me more special than him?" she said. Sheila wasn't in love while her husband cheated on her. But Sheila loved. The first twelve years of her marriage, collectively, was a cross, she said. "And I carried it."

Love Is Always Your Job

"I love him," I said to a friend about a guy.

She widened her eyes. "You *love*, love him?" she asked.

"I *love*, love him," I said.

The gravity of what I admitted would shift when, a month later, he and I discovered the truth about each other. He—a Protestant—was never going to marry a Catholic woman, and I was never going to leave the Catholic Church. We agreed to call it quits because we both understood such an impasse would not resolve itself with time. Love renders some people able to live with their impasses, but some impasses render others unable to commit.

One night, after the relationship ended, I sat in the dark in front of the TV, crying with a glass of water in my hand. I laughed, too, because the TV's light behind the amber glass made the water look a lot like scotch on the rocks. I really don't drink. I especially don't drink scotch. I sipped my water and agreed to feel what I felt: anger, loss, and pain. It had taken twenty-six years to meet a man I wanted to *love*, love. How long would I have to wait to meet another?

I wallowed, miserably unaware of what the Church says about love, that it is "the fundamental and innate vocation of every human being" (CCC 2392). I had loved, and I had lost. But does that mean my life doesn't align with my vocation anymore, or does it mean I'm preoccupied by living it out in only one way?

I wanted to get married because married people get to love. And married people *do* get to love. But they don't have a monopoly on love. What I hadn't grasped yet was that love takes multiple forms, and all of them require sacrifice.

"Love," for married people, "is in the tasks that become redundant," said Jeanine Spano. "It's saying our morning prayers together and missing it when we don't. [It's] taking turns taking care of our two toddlers," even while tired.

Love is "not letting things fester, not letting anger build up," and "expressing emotions through good communication," said Matt Cullum.

"Love," for single people, "is going to a friend's for a visit and in the process, throwing a football with one of their kids because it makes the child happy," said Paul Catalanotto, a single Catholic schoolteacher.

"Love is sharing my umbrella with my brother, even when I'm mad at him. Love is when I am a shoulder to cry on for my best friend," said Mary-Catherine Donaghy, a single college student.

"Love is actions that require you to give parts of yourself, even if you'd rather not," said Serah Okechukwu, a single college student.

Love "is not a swooning, honeymoon thing where I giggle like a school girl. This is the love that says God has seen me at my worst and remains in me and with me," said Sister Teresa MacDonald.

Love is "giving myself to God and his people. I don't look to be fulfilled. In the giving is the fulfillment," said Father Salvatore DeStefano.

"Love is surrender," said Father Daniel O'Mullane.

And all of us can do that every day.

Self-Control

A Response to the Contraception Controversy

"For God did not give us a spirit of cowardice but rather of power and love and self-control."

—*2 Timothy 1:7*

I hate debating. The disdain I harbor for it is so deep that I prefer to agree to disagree with people whose points of view and mine are so different that a discussion could engender an entertaining debate. When I share what I believe—even if it is controversial—I do so not to persuade the unconvinced but to inform the curious or comfort kindred spirits who might otherwise feel alone. If what I express happens to elicit a change of heart or mind in somebody with whom I'd historically disagree, I consider it a bonus.

The demise of my relationship with debating started during my sophomore year of high school. On the whiteboard at the front of a portable classroom, the only other Catholic kid in the class—Julie, whom our teacher called "the scribe"—wrote our classmates' prayer requests each morning. Then I—whose nickname was "the prayer warrior"—prayed about them aloud. The routine, a memory I totally cherish, represents coexistence at a school that resisted it. Julie and I were out of place a lot in our private, Protestant school. Over and over, I found myself in theological debates (usually with teachers) about controversial subjects, such as salvation, the saints, and birth control.

The morning that birth control came up in class, I delivered an ardent, impromptu speech, inspired by why the Catholic Church doesn't condone the use of contraception—or at least what I understood of its reasons. I banged my fists on the desk and shouted with conviction and comedic timing: "I don't believe in birth control. I believe in self-control!" And I meant it. But we cracked up, and somebody changed the subject. The subject, however, has come up again and again ever since.

On a Saturday night as an undergrad, I took a long walk with a friend and her brother along dark streets in suburban Spring Hill, Florida. Upon our return to their house, we ordered a pizza—our reward for having burned a bunch of calories. Over dinner, we—all single, then—discussed marriage and sex, which is when my friend declared: "When I get married, I'm definitely using contraception." She said, "I don't want ten kids."

Though my interest in debating had waned a lot already, I used what little of it was left to concoct an argument. "Contraception is poison," I said, while I pushed away my plate. I braced for a debate. My friend's brother took her side. The science behind the patches and pills makes them safe, he said, not poisonous. Besides, my friend added, "For the first few years of marriage, your husband's going to want to have sex every day."

My friend's point illustrates why the Church *needs* to make the points it does. A person's urge to have sex a lot does not necessitate contraception; it necessitates chastity—a sustained, lifelong effort to put the other's needs first. But my friend didn't know that. She didn't know, back then, that submission in marriage is supposed to be mutual—that it isn't a burden, but the relief of a burden, if each spouse can be trusted to make decisions in the best interest of the other; that abstinence before marriage doesn't mean a wedding marks the start of a sexual free-for-all, but that abstinence before marriage is good practice for sacrifice *in* marriage.

The use of contraception is an exercise in control, but the kind of control it promotes—control of fertility—makes another kind of control obsolete: *self*-control. Self-control requires us to rise above our urges. It facilitates personal growth and fosters maturity, but it isn't a priority in our culture, which is enamored by having its cake and eating it, too.

While some women are prescribed the Pill for health reasons rather than to avoid pregnancy (which, for the record, is not contrary to Church teaching), most people who use contraception use it to separate the two primary purposes of sex: bonding and babies. This is so sex can be casual, or because the partners aren't prepared to raise a child (or an additional child), or because the world is over-populated. But is the problem "too many babies," or is it "too many people having sex"?

Is Contraception "Health Care"?

In 2012, Catholic bishops called attention to a regulation in President Barack Obama's Affordable Care Act, which would require Catholic institutions, including universities, to pay for coverage of contraception. A coalition of students from Catholic universities called a press conference at the National Press Club in Washington, DC, and in it, they decried the Church's resistance to compliance with the regulation and urged the Church to take a hint from the women who identify as Catholic but use contraception.

In 2013, a letter from the Boston College administration told the student-led organization BC Students for Sexual Health (BCSSH) to stop distributing condoms on campus or else be disciplined. As word spread about the warning, the organization posted letters on its website, many of which it received from Boston College students and alumni, expressing sympathy for the group, support for the distribution of contraception on college campuses (including Catholic ones), and anger at the Catholic Church for not relenting.

People who don't agree with what the Church teaches about contraception express their concerns with sincerity. Their concerns are underlain by passions for justice and sexual health. The Church is passionate about justice and sexual health, too. But each camp defines "justice" and "sexual health" in fundamentally different ways. A conversation devolves if we don't acknowledge how different the lenses are through which we each look at the world.

Like Turkey for Christmas

A day or two before Christmas break, fellow high-school students and I congregated in our English teacher's classroom, where we discussed our holiday plans. My teacher, who would prepare a feast for her family on Christmas day, told us her frozen turkey already was thawing at home in her kitchen sink.

"A *turkey?*" I shook my head. "Who eats *turkey* on Christmas?" I laughed out loud at the absurdity and scanned the room for signs of solidarity from my now painfully quiet classmates.

Finally, one of them spoke. "Uh, *everyone* eats turkey on Christmas. . . ."

Another one had to ask: "What do *you* eat on Christmas?"

"I eat lasagna on Christmas," I said. "I thought everyone did."

I discovered—disconcertingly later in life than the average Italian kid—that Italian food for Christmas is not a universal tradition. But until the revelation in a freshman English class, I saw Christmas dinner egocentrically. In my world, Christmas dinner is lasagna. If Christmas dinner is lasagna, turkey is *not* Christmas dinner. Turkey is absurd.

In the same way, egocentric thought in the contraception conversation results in opposing sides that appeal to the same ideals, using the same terms, while defining them very differently.

In a letter, for instance, posted on the BCSSH website, a representative of H*yas for Choice, an organization led by Georgetown University students, wrote: "Creating an environment where sexual health is promoted and celebrated should be a fundamental tenet of any university that respects the well-being of its students."

The Church agrees, and it teaches that sexual health involves the preservation of all the purposes of sex—which protects the body from disease, prevents one person from using another as a means to an end, and respects the dignity innate in each of us.

In another BCSSH letter, Martha (Marty) Walz, president and chief executive officer of the Planned Parenthood League of Massachusetts, wrote, "With STD rates rising among people under age twenty-five, empowering young women and men to make healthy decisions should be a top priority for all of us."

The Church agrees with that, too. But according to the Church, chastity empowers us; contraception doesn't. The Church's opposition to the use of contraception is *part* of its aim to promote sexual health. Within (not despite) its opposition to the distribution and use of contraception, it *seeks* to empower young people to make healthy choices. For the Catholic Church, this means guiding young adults toward experiencing authentic love, not through sexual self-expression but through giving themselves, 100 percent, in loving service to family, friends, and community, while rejecting contraception and embracing chastity as a means to true sexual health.

In one letter, a Boston College student named Kate wrote that by not allowing condoms to be distributed to students on campus, the administration is jeopardizing students' health. In another letter, Phil (Boston College class of '72) wrote that in banning the distribution of condoms on campus, Catholicism exposes "young adults to . . . lethal diseases."

But is it actually Boston College's fault if a student contracts a sexually transmitted infection, or is it the fault of the adults who consented to the sexual activity that transmitted it? Objectively, the Boston College administration ordered BCSSH to stop giving out condoms on campus. Subjectively, the move was regarded by its detractors to be the school's reckless rejection of its responsibility to protect its students from harm. However, according to the ideals of the supporters of Boston College's action, the move was evidence of the school's resolve to uphold a teaching of the Church designed, in part, to protect us.

The Church and Sexual Health

The people who don't agree with what the Church teaches about contraception don't need debates; they need examples. They don't need reasons why their way doesn't work but reasons why our way does. We have to express with our lives why we choose this viewpoint despite how widely rejected it is. The backlash when the bishops spoke up in 2012 bothered me, as did the outcry after Boston College called out the students who violated a rule. What I watched—college kids, and some of them nominally Catholic, demanding free condoms on Catholic campuses and berating the Church for not abandoning its ideals on behalf of a faction—resulted in profound concern and stress-induced acne. I didn't (and probably still don't) always have the grace to say this nicely: the people who most often misrepresent the Catholic Church are Catholics.

A widely circulated quote attributed to Archbishop Fulton Sheen says, "There are not one hundred people in the United States who hate the Catholic Church. But there are millions who hate what they wrongly perceive the Catholic Church to be." I learned, in the wake of the widely publicized contraception controversy, that the general public perceives the Catholic Church's rejection of contraception as equivalent to a rejection of sexual health.

But it isn't.

"Empowering young women and men to make healthy decisions" is, in fact, among the Church's highest priorities. "Do you not know that your body is a temple of the Holy Spirit within you, whom you have from God?" (1 Cor 6:19). We are called as Christians to take care of our bodies, which, as we profess in the Apostles' Creed, we believe will

resurrect and reunite with our souls someday after death. Do
we need a better reason to take care of them than that? The
objection to the use of contraception doesn't stifle a young
person's ability to make healthy choices, but contraception
does. With it, a partner's "intentions are thereby diverted
from the person and directed to mere enjoyment; 'the person as co-creator of love' disappears and there remains only
'the partner in an erotic experience.' Nothing could be more
incompatible with the proper ends of the act of love."[21] The
incorrect perception that the Church does not stand in favor
of healthy choices is indicative not solely of the differences
in the opinions of the general public and the Church, but of
the need to clarify what the Church actually teaches.

The Church and Contraception: Common Misconceptions

- *The Catholic Church believes sex is solely for procreation.*

  Nope! Sex, according to the Church, has "procreative
  and unitive purposes" (CCC 2351). It's not solely for
  makin' babies but is also for bonding with a spouse.

- *The Catholic Church doesn't want women to enjoy sex.*

  God designed sex to be pleasurable, but pleasure is not
  the primary purpose of sex. "Sexual pleasure is morally disordered when sought for itself, isolated from its
  procreative and unitive purposes" (CCC 2351). Sexual
  pleasure, for women and for men, is a Church-approved
  bonus when achieved in conjunction with chaste sex.

- *The Catholic Church expects people to have a bunch of kids.*

  This is not necessarily true. The Church expects married
  couples to be open to the transmission of life in sex, to
  give our whole selves to our spouses, and to accept our
  spouses wholly (which includes their fertility). In *Love*

and Responsibility, Karol Wojtyla (who would become St. John Paul II) wrote, "If the possibility of parenthood is deliberately excluded from marital relations, the character of the relationship between the partners automatically changes. The change is away from unification in love and in the direction of mutual, or rather bilateral, 'enjoyment.'" . . . Willing acceptance of parenthood serves to break down the reciprocal egoism— (or the egoism of one party at which the other connives) —behind which lurks the will to exploit the person."[22]

- *The Church opposes contraception because the more Catholics there are, the more power the Church has.*

  False; instead, the Church teaches that "the innate language that expresses the total reciprocal self-giving of husband and wife is overlaid, through contraception, by an objectively contradictory language, namely, that of not giving oneself totally to the other" (CCC 2370). The opposition to contraception isn't a power play. It's rooted in the preservation of the purposes of sex, which involve one partner's total acceptance of the other, including his or her fertility.

- *The Church thinks God alone is supposed to be in charge of family size.*

  Nope. The Church teaches, "With regard to the biological processes, responsible parenthood means an awareness of, and respect for, their proper functions" (*Humanae Vitae* 10). The Church doesn't say we can't plan the sizes of our own families; it says we can't turn off our fertility. We create our families in collaboration with God.

The purpose of sex, according to the Church, is equal parts procreation and unity. We believe humans are not designed to have sex because sex is pleasurable, but to create a pleasurable sexual relationship in a marriage. We believe sex is designed for uniting spouses and creating families. I grew up in a culture that disagrees—a culture that says sex is primarily for personal pleasure, that it is only for procreation if you want it to be, and that if your method of family planning doesn't involve contraception, you'll turn into the Duggars.

There is a sense of urgency among the people in the general public to use contraception. "Use it, or be irresponsible." The uproar after Boston College told students not to distribute condoms on campus was underlain by fear—fear of lives uprooted by pregnancy or by the transmission of infection. I think sometimes people believe Catholics oppose contraception because we don't consider babies or STIs to be big deals. But it's just the opposite. We think they are deals so big that we ought to reserve sex for the context of a lifelong union, safe for babies and safe from disease.

Access to contraception will not eliminate the possibility of conceiving a child with someone to whom you aren't committed or when one or both of you isn't prepared to raise a family. Foregoing sex, on the other hand, will. What inspires one person to use a condom inspires another to abstain from sex. The Church has good reasons to require the latter, even beyond its effectiveness and safety. God created sex for marriage, for two people to reflect God's life-giving creativity and love to the whole world.

Instead, the world uses contraception to make sex "safe"—theoretically controlled and predictable, devoid of danger or regret. In the process, we are reduced to little more than animals, who can't *not* act on urges, who don't have to consider our actions' consequences and implications. But we were created able to think before we act, and sex is supposed to be so sacred that danger and regret in it aren't possible. When sex is what sex is supposed to be, it requires a person to embrace every part of his or her partner. It requires us to relinquish control, which gives us a reason to acknowledge the magnitude of what we're doing. Out of respect for God and the beloved, married love calls a person to embrace the potential that sex might make a man a dad and a woman a mom. When sex is what sex is supposed to be, we are perpetually pointed toward something other than self. We are given permission (and a reason to drum up the courage) to consider that sex is greater, and more powerful, than "it feels good."

For sex to be what it's supposed to be requires chastity, which requires abstinence from sex outside of marriage. In an informal survey I conducted of people who oppose the Church's stance on contraception, multiple respondents wrote that God gave us brains and we should use them— that by thinking critically we can decide to take advantage of contraception, in or outside a marriage, when we aren't prepared to raise a child. On one hand, my survey participants are correct: God indeed did give us brains with which we can think critically. But how critically have we thought when pregnancy isn't an option but we can't conclude that abstinence—the only 100 percent effective way to prevent a pregnancy—is a good idea?

When we apply critical thought to contraception, we also can conclude that it potentially strips sex of its purposes: procreation and unity. Contraception has created an environment in which we have to be protected from our partners, instead of an environment in which picking partners with whom we know we are safe is important to us. It creates barriers, separating the people who are engaging in an activity designed to unite them.

Natural Family Planning

Ennie and Cana Hickman live in Houston, Texas, and have been married for thirteen years. Both thirty-four, Ennie and Cana are missionaries for Adore Ministries, a Christian outreach organization. As practicing Catholics who have never used contraception, they have six children: Madeline, twelve; Dominic, ten; Sophia, eight; Avila, six; Lucia, three; and Quinn, one. They started their marriage using the symptothermal model of natural family planning (NFP) and now use the Creighton model.[23] We chatted once about their choosing NFP.

Why do you use NFP?

Ennie: We had grown up knowing that if God wanted to bless us with children, we should be open to that. We knew we didn't want to bring contraception into our relationship. NFP offered a good way for us to live the morals we were raised up in.

What are the pros of NFP?

Ennie: It's definitely brought us closer as a couple. Everybody will always say the key to a good relationship is communication, and there's no greater way to communicate. You have to talk about it. The greatest pro for me is there's discipline to it. You come into these periods of time where you're fasting [from sex]. The misconception may be that the sex is not good. I get to date my wife again. It makes sex better. It's like fasting before a great big meal. That meal is so much more satisfying. The sex is great. I was hanging out with some guys and they straight up asked me, "How often do you have sex with your wife?" And I told them, "On average, two or three times a week." These guys almost fell out of their chairs. It blew their minds that we had a healthy sex life.

Cana: Within seconds, we can try to achieve a pregnancy. There's no IUD to take out, no pill to get off of. You're in tune with your body. It's a natural way to approach fertility.

And the cons?

Ennie: The discipline. I love discipline, but it sucks. You have to sacrifice. You have to abstain.

Cana: It's a simple concept—identifying your fertility and abstaining—but it's not necessarily very easy. Some women have regular [cycles] and some women don't. You happen to be talking to someone who doesn't.

A lot of people who use NFP have a lot of kids. Does that mean NFP isn't effective?

Cana: It's an absolutely false assumption but an understandable one. People who use NFP are generally more open to having children. It works just fine [to prevent pregnancies] if you use it properly.

Ennie: In general, people who have a lot of children using NFP probably wanted a lot of children. I've always wanted a lot of kids.

❀

The "Up Side" of NFP

Does the Church expect couples (as one survey respondent wrote) to have "a baby a year"? No. Within marriage, Catholic couples are encouraged to use Natural Family Planning (NFP), monitoring a woman's signs of fertility, to achieve or avoid pregnancy. If the goal is to avoid pregnancy, the couple abstains from sex when the signs say the female is fertile. The couple has sex when the signs say she isn't.

While some object to having to abstain from sex periodically, other couples find their relationships strengthened by NFP. When a couple uses NFP, a husband gets to know his wife's body in a way he otherwise wouldn't, and both spouses experience total self-giving in fertile and infertile periods alike. Both premarital abstinence and periodic abstinence within marriage cultivate essential qualities and skills that strengthen every part of a marriage, such as commitment and communication.

Consistently living out these qualities and skills across contexts is what makes us good at them, as illustrated in an episode of *Boy Meets World*. Main character Cory—then in seventh grade—turns to his teacher, Mr. Turner, for help making a difficult decision. The decision Cory later makes backfires on him, and he returns to Mr. Turner. Their conversation goes like this:

Cory: "I made the wrong decision."

Mr. Turner: "I could've told you that."

Cory [agitated]: "Why didn't you?"

Mr. Turner: "You don't listen in class. You're gonna listen in life?"

A life is not a life of virtue if we pick and choose the contexts in which to practice virtue. It can be tempting to pass on practicing virtue when practicing it doesn't feel important. We tell ourselves we can slack off in one context and our overall work ethic won't suffer, or that we can lie in one context and our honesty in other contexts won't waver. We tell ourselves we can zone out in one context and our listening skills won't deteriorate altogether.

But if an aspiring entrepreneur won't work hard when she's flipping burgers, is she going to work hard when she starts a business? If a guy isn't honest with his friends, will he tell his wife the truth? Aspiring to embody a particular quality in a particular context is not nearly as important as whether you discipline yourself to cultivate and practice that quality at all times and in all circumstances. If we are unwilling to commit to periodic abstinence, or to communicate with a spouse enough for NFP to work, a marriage is bound to suffer in other areas, too. If we *are* willing, the result won't solely help us be better spouses but—when the time is right—to be better parents, too.

What's the Point of All of This, Really?

Why be open to procreation in a culture that doesn't require it? Why practice NFP when you could just buy condoms? Because openness to life, parenthood, and NFP helps us to do part of what we are all called to do while we are here on earth: love.

In grad school, I sat in a circle of students once in a counseling theories class. Pen in hand and a self-inventory worksheet in front of me, I pondered the question at the top of the paper: "What did you learn about love from how your parents treated you?" This is what I wrote: *Love requires trust (in multiple ways). Trustworthiness was expected of me, not as a condition of love but as a function of it. Love is tough. When I am loved, I am held to high standards, expected to be the best I can, and not enabled to do whatever is less than my best.*

I think about this a lot, as a daughter and sister and friend, as a single woman, and as a potential wife and mom. This love we can give by being open to life is not about one person requiring another to change (from fertile to infertile, for instance). It is not about manipulating a person into being who he or she isn't, or who you'd like him or her to be (that isn't love, either). It is not about having unreasonable expectations (like when my goal was to find—nay, be *found* by—a Catholic chiropractor who has dreadlocks and a Scottish accent).

Instead, it is about *ti voglio bene*, as Edward Sri wrote in *Men, Women and the Mystery of Love*.[24] The phrase is Italian for "I love you," but translated literally, Sri wrote, it is "I wish you good" or "I want what is good for you." This love is fostered in marriage and involves sacrifice—willing sacrifice—because when you become a loving spouse and parent, creating a healthy environment for your spouse and children becomes more important to you than always feeling gratified. This love is about not putting yourself between your kid and reasonable consequences for his or her behavior (if you always save your children, they don't learn). It's about not spoiling your kid, even if it makes you sad when your kid doesn't get what he or she wants, and even if your kid's response to "no" irritates the snot out of you (because kids who are given everything become adults who don't want to do anything). This love expects the beloved to reach the bar (of integrity, responsibility, chastity) and doesn't lower it for them, because to lower the bar for somebody—while easy for you—is to contribute to the maintenance of his or her status quo.

This love—though tough—is about being there for the beloved through his or her growing pains rather than vetoing his or her growth so you don't have to witness the pain. It is a love that makes the world a better place. It carves out of the culture of death a culture of life.

chapter 7

Purity
Not Your Responsibility

"But God demonstrates his own love
toward us, in that while we were yet sin-
ners, Christ died for us. Much more then,
having now been justified by his blood,
we shall be saved from the wrath of God
through him. For if while we were enemies
we were reconciled to God through the
death of his Son, much more, having been
reconciled, we shall be saved by his life."

—Romans 5:8–10

The preacher passed the cup of clear water to a young
adult in the congregation, who spit in it, according to the
preacher's instructions. The first young adult passed it to the

second, and the second to another, and so on, so everybody
in the room had a turn to spit.

"Some boys horked and honked their worst into that
cup while everyone laughed," wrote Sarah Bessey, author of
Jesus Feminist, who recounted the experience in an essay she
wrote in 2013 for *A Deeper Story*.[25] The purpose of the cup
of water was to illustrate what the preacher thought would
happen to the young adults who decided not to save sex for
marriage. He held up the cup, after all the spit had clouded
it, and asked, "Who wants to drink this?"

"[Everyone] in the crowd made barfing noises," Sarah
wrote, and the preacher continued to preach. "This is what
you are like if you have sex before marriage. . . . You are
asking your future husband or wife to drink this cup.'" Sarah's face turned red, she wrote, because she—then nineteen
years old—was sexually experienced. If the preacher was
right, she was like the cup of spit water. The preacher's sermon was supposed to encourage the young congregants
to "stay pure for marriage," but for Sarah, it did not result
in an interest in the pursuit or maintenance of purity. It led
instead to her struggle to see herself as worth more than
"damaged goods."

Lots of stories akin to Sarah's have been shared in the
Christian blogosphere, often by young adults who grew
up in churches at the same time I did, whose introductions
to abstinence, chastity, and purity inadvertently blurred
the lines that belong between them. Sermons designed to
encourage a way of life that aligns with real love . . . didn't.
And that isn't because kids weren't listening to them. Kids
were listening, but the words their ministers used and the
contexts in which they used them achieved unfortunate
results.

In a blog post called "When Purity Culture Hurts Men,
Too," author and blogger Preston Yancey writes about being

thirteen years old, sitting with a red "True Love Waits" card in front of him at church. He signed it and considered the card a sign of his "pledge to God and my genitals that I would never lust again."[26]

"I believe this lasted about an evening," he wrote. And "when it was over with, when the pledge had been broken . . . I wondered what the point of it all had been. Was it simply a setup to shame me, a guaranteed trap I would stumble right into as quickly as I had raised the pen to promise that I would never compromise myself or another man's future wife?" He had learned at church, it seems, that his promise to save sex for marriage would require a rejection of lust. However, he could not control what wasn't within his power, and that lust was not within his power was a concept he learned at church. So his lust "was her fault," he thought at thirteen. "She chose to dress the part of my desires. I was only being natural."

Preston doesn't buy that anymore.

Paul is a Catholic youth minister who intentionally doesn't use analogies like the one in Sarah Bessey's story when he teaches adolescents about abstinence, chastity, and purity. He met a girl twenty years ago at his youth group, when—though she wasn't Catholic—she attended with a friend. She was "fifteen, maybe," he said, when her parents caught her having sex with a boyfriend. "They brought her to their pastor, who brought her in front of the entire congregation, and they all screamed insults and names at her during a service," he said—names such as whore and slut.

She shared her story with Paul and later showed up at his church a couple more times. But after that, Paul said, she "never popped up at youth group again." He thinks about her all the time, he said. He still prays for her "because there's no telling where she's ended up. If I could verbalize the hurt in that girl's eyes . . ."

In early adolescence, Carolynn—now a wife and blogger—learned "purity was keeping yourself from having sex until you were married. . . . This is all I knew purity to be," she said. "I thought there would be some marked difference on the skin, the face of a person" who had sex outside of marriage.

After high school, Carolynn dated and eventually had sex with her boyfriend. "I realized I was now impure," she said. "I remember looking in the mirror to see if anything had changed. If *I* had changed. But I looked the same." That confused her, she said. "I really wanted to be a good girl, but I also wanted to have sex. And all I heard from adults in my life was that sex was wrong, wrong, wrong. I . . . wondered if the stain on myself was permanent, or if the whole purity thing was a lie," she said. No one she knew could clarify purity's definition.

Arguably, lots of church leaders have tried. But as evidenced by the aforementioned stories, some of their tries have failed. Using condemnatory, shame-based sermons, many first have encouraged purity, then have put children in charge of maintaining it and have implied a person's worth is wrapped up in it—all without ever clearly defining it. The analogies the preacher used in Sarah Bessey's story have been used in other churches, too. Starting a marriage with sexual experience, some of us were told, is like giving somebody a pair of dirty shoes with holey soles instead of a brand new pair, or giving somebody "ABC gum" (already been chewed). There is no mercy or grace in that message. But a message devoid of mercy and grace is not a Gospel message.

To compare a person who is sexually experienced with spit water or old shoes or used gum reduces him or her from a person whose value is intrinsic to an object nobody wants. The truth is that nothing, and I mean *nothing*, a person does or doesn't do can change his or her value. The spit, shoe, and gum analogies imply that there is no turning back, that people who have had nonmarital sex are worth less than the people who haven't, that a person whose past doesn't align with what he or she believes now will never find (or make) a good marriage partner. But God is merciful. He knows we stumble and fall and that we make choices that have consequences that hurt ourselves and others. He forgives, and he gives us the grace to start over. This is the message the Church and its representatives need to present to youth and young adults. Shaming and making threats are not the solution; hope is.

How Should We Discuss Sex in Youth Groups?

"We can't talk about sin unless we first talk about love. [Damage done by purity culture] is a result of preaching the horrors of sin before we preach love and mercy. Love isn't about fear. Scare tactics don't work with youth. Modern youth aren't afraid of hell or death in general. Once they encounter Christ, his love and mercy are so much bigger and so much more effective than any scare tactic.

"The bottom line with all youth ministry is that we should never be talking at the youth. It's important to approach it from the perspective of 'we are all in this journey together.' Talk about the gift of sexuality and how it is used properly and how it is abused.

"When we fall short, we must run to the sacrament of Reconciliation. We have a God who forgives and when he forgives, we have new life. We must go forward and strive to be chaste from that moment on."

—Jason Carter, youth minister
St. Frances Cabrini Catholic Church
Spring Hill, Florida

"Before you can dive into those topics, you have to build a relationship with [with a teen]. The idea is these teenagers are used to me being in conversation with them. . . . There is such a deeper purpose to human sexuality. While I think a kid can understand similes and metaphors, it's not complete. They don't actually describe what you're talking about. [The analogies don't say] that sexuality is a gift, not something to be feared, but to be protected and developed.

"In the nineties, it was like the whole 'just say no' culture. That only works if you give somebody an alternative to say yes to."

—Paul Hood, youth minister
Our Lady of Prompt Succor Catholic Church
Alexandria, Louisiana

Purity Culture

While I wrote my first *Times* essay about saving sex, I rummaged at home through a drawer I rarely open, in search of an old wallet I never use. When I found it, I opened it to discover what I hoped I would: a business card stuck in a credit-card slot, etched with a pledge I signed in high school:

> Believing that my sexuality is a gift from God, I make a commitment to God, myself, my family, and friends to use the gift of my body and sexuality to bring honor, respect, and dignity to both God and myself. I choose to live a chaste life both now and in the future vocation to which God calls me.

I did not remember then where I signed it (and I still don't). But when I signed it on July 1 in 2002, I became one of countless American teenagers who promised in pen to reserve sex as something to experience solely with a spouse.

In the essay I wrote, I referenced the card, and—even though the word "purity" isn't anywhere on it—I called it a "purity pledge." After the essay appeared in print, a reader called it out in an e-mail. "Why is it called a 'purity pledge'? Why not a 'virginity pledge'? Are those of us who have sex without marriage 'impure'?" he wrote. "Why insult us because we disagree with your views? You can call me a 'non-virgin,' but not impure, please."

I had neither the time nor the expertise to actually answer his questions, so I sent him a generic response "Sorry to hear the pledge offends you," I wrote, "but I appreciate your reading my essay."

He wrote back: "The pledge does not offend me, the terminology does. It implies that non-virgins are impure." I ignored the e-mail, and forgot about it, until I stumbled upon a discussion of purity culture on Christian blogs.

As I read bloggers' posts about the pursuit of a better sexual ethic, their qualms with purity, virginity, and chastity sermons surprised me. In my quest to introduce the general public to chastity, I had drawn criticism about it from people—non-Christians, I'd assumed, such as the guy offended by use of the word "purity"—who didn't share my point of view. But why were similar criticisms showing up in posts on *Christian* blogs? There *is* no better ethic than chastity, I thought, and we really *ought* to talk about it. But the posts showcased a side of the purity conversation to which I hadn't had much exposure. That side featured poorly worded purity pledges and super awkward purity balls; and teens being berated by youth pastors, being told sex is bad, and becoming adults who have had to undo the damage all of it did. The bloggers who spoke up about it, many of whom identify as Christian, called it "purity culture."

Purity culture, according to the founder of the No Shame Movement—an Internet platform people use to help others unlearn what they've learned from purity culture—"encourages policing [sexual] thoughts and actions that are a part of human nature, instead of teaching people to embrace them in a way that is healthy." The founder, who goes by LP in order to maintain anonymity, believes purity is a myth. "I don't think it's a real thing that anyone should strive for," she said. "People should be encouraged to embrace sexuality in a healthy way that works for them, respect one another, and have autonomy over their own bodies." As LP understands it, purity culture says a person who is pure "refrains from non-approved sexual activity."

But purity culture is described in other ways, too. In an essay called "The Vulgar Face of Purity Culture" on *Huffington Post*, Anne Almasy wrote:

> The core of purity culture was that my mind didn't matter, my personality didn't matter, my dreams and desires and goals didn't matter—if my shorts were too short. Or if I wore a bikini, if I kissed a boy, if I kissed a GIRL, if I shook my bootie when I danced, if I ever-ever-ever had sex for any reason whatsoever before I was married.[27]

In another article, Jonalyn Grace Fincher points out that "purity is one of the only places Christians treat sin as undegreed. If you lose your virginity," she wrote, purity culture says "you're beyond rehabilitation."[28]

On ConvergentBooks.com, Kendall Davis says, "Virgins were said to be pure, while girls who gave in were likened to a destroyed rose, a cup of spit, or a candy bar that had been tasted and touched by several people."[29]

Purity culture doesn't teach young people the value of chastity or the grace of God. It teaches that sexual activity outside of marriage so irreversibly hurts us that there truly isn't any turning back. While some things really *can't* be undone—you can't erase the sex you've had, or the pregnancy, or the baby, or the abortion, or some STIs, or emotional wounds—we still have to consider: do we help people by scaring them, or do we help them by telling them the truth?

The truth is that sex *can* result in babies or STIs or emotional wounds. But the following is also true:

- We are loved and of infinite value, regardless of what we do or don't do.

- God doesn't stop loving or liking us when we sin.

- Chastity is not synonymous with virginity or abstinence.

- Participating in the sacraments can be a healing experience. God uses the sacraments to deliver the grace with which we can start over.

- Some people are coerced or forced into sexual experiences—experiences they neither wanted nor knew how to handle. People who are coerced or forced into sexual encounters have not sinned. They've been sinned against, and God wants them to experience help and healing.

- Having had a consensual sexual experience outside of marriage does not mean your life is ruined.

- Forgiveness is the path to healing after every kind of sin.

The following story is a good example of how having the whole truth can change somebody's life.

The Confession

Not long ago, as a friend's wedding date approached, she—in her thirties—wasn't sure she deserved to be happy or whether her marriage would last. She had been in several previous relationships that left deep scars. She *wanted* a happy marriage, though, and thought if she talked with somebody about her past, she might be able to get married without regrets. She decided, then, to go to confession at an old, country parish in preparation to receive the sacrament of Matrimony. She tells the rest of the story best:

> The church had seen better days. The floorboards were noticeably lighter than the pews from so much foot traffic. A wizened old priest slowly made his way into the middle compartment of the ancient confessional.
>
> There was no one else in the sanctuary, which was just fine with me. I figured I was going to be in there for a while. I had never talked about these things before and wasn't sure how long it would take.
>
> Getting down on the kneeler, I just opened up about everything I had held inside for more than a decade: The older "boyfriend" who held me down as a teenager and forced himself on me and later abandoned me. The young Catholic man who had helped me recover from this painful relationship, who I later rejected out of ignorance and fear. On and on I went, naming nearly two decades of heartache, brokenness, regret, and anxiety.
>
> I'm not sure how long I was in that confessional, getting it all off my chest. But when I stopped speaking . . . there was silence on the other side of the screen. I was a little scared. Had I shocked the elderly priest? Or maybe bored him so he fell asleep?

At last I heard him clear his throat. Then he said the most amazing words: "Oh, my daughter. You have been so terribly, terribly wronged," he began. With a voice full of gentle compassion, he reminded me of the Father who had never abandoned me, who had seen my struggle and wept with me in my pain. Then he blessed me and sent me off to begin my new life. There were still plenty of bags to unpack, but the messiest ones were in the hands of God.

Unfortunately, not every preacher, priest, or congregation points people toward this sort of grace or toward our intrinsic value. But that this grace exists, and that all of us can access it, is what everyone needs to know. We need to know we are not at fault if somebody sins against us. We need to know what we do or what's done to us cannot change how much we're worth. Preachers, priests, and congregations need to create spaces that are so safe, that in them, people who discover a need to modify their behavior can discover it without being told how they've behaved determines how good they are. We need spaces so safe we can learn in them to forgive ourselves and to receive God's forgiveness. When the spaces we create aren't safe for that, we are part of the culture decried above and described in Jessica Valenti's book *The Purity Myth*.

Unmasking the "Purity Myth"

The first time I saw a Jessica Valenti book, I scowled at it and stuck it back between other books on a shelf at the bookstore. I had judged it by its cover, which had *The Purity Myth: How America's Obsession with Virginity Is Hurting Young Women* scrawled across the middle, in white letters. But eventually, as a result of curiosity and exposure to the detractors of purity culture, I ordered a copy. Albeit unlikely—based solely on its title—that I would like the book or agree with what's written in it, it turned out to be among the most important books I've read.

Valenti is a feminist, and in the book she criticizes what she calls the "purity myth" for shaming women who have sex outside of marriage; for promoting hierarchical relationships, in which men are always authoritative and women are always submissive; and for perpetuating the myths that men are *so* sexual their urges can't be controlled and that women aren't sexual at all. Before I read it, I thought the book—which I now count as one of my favorites—would discount abstinence, chastity, and purity. And, I discovered, it does. But the parts of each that Valenti decried are not associated with the chastity I practice—they are associated with misconceptions of it. Valenti made a lot of good points—points with which I agree: That purity balls, which are formal father-daughter dances in which daughters pledge their virginity to their dads, are unnecessary; that the word "purity" is widely misused to imply that a person who has had sex is impure. That use of the word "purity" potentially creates or maintains the belief that sex is bad—a belief that, when deep-seated, is not so easy to shake on a wedding night.

However, throughout the book, Valenti used the words "abstinence," "chastity," and "purity" interchangeably. She used the phrases "purity myth" and "virginity movement" interchangeably, too. That she didn't differentiate between them perpetuates misconceptions of each.

"In [one virginity-movement writer's] worldview," Valenti wrote, "women are naturally modest and chaste; if we're sexual at all, it's because of outside influences."[30] But real chastity doesn't imply asexuality.

"What's the difference between venerating women for being [sexually desirable] . . . and putting them on a purity pedestal?" Valenti wrote. "In both cases, women's worth is contingent upon their ability to please men and to shape their sexual identities around what men want."[31] But anybody who treats anybody else as though his or her value is not intrinsic is not practicing chastity.

According to Valenti, what the movement is "striving for is not progressive change, but a return to 'traditional' norms and a time when porn—widely defined as seemingly anything that's not women in head-to-toe prairie dresses and anything less chaste than hand-holding—existed but was hidden from view and not discussed."[32] Anything less chaste than handholding? The line implies that the closer a couple gets to sexual intercourse, the less chaste they are being. That would only be true if chastity ended when a person has sex. But chastity is not supposed to end, ever, not even at marriage.

I wholeheartedly agree with Valenti when she points out the damage done by a belief system that aligns better with purity culture than with the Gospel. But I disagree with the implication that chastity necessarily involves adherence to the beliefs that perpetuate the purity myth—one of many myths, really, in the book.

How Should We Discuss Sex with Kids?

Dr. Dae Sheridan, the sex therapist who taught my human sexuality class in grad school, tells us on her website, DrDae. com, how to talk sex with kids. Here's an adapted version of her advice:

- *Strive to eliminate the concept of "the talk."* Remember "*the* talk"? It provided you with everything you needed to know about sex, love, and intimate relationships, right? Ha! Me neither. Sexuality education is not a one-time speech about "the birds and the bees," but a series

of age-appropriate teachings and ongoing conversa-
tions with our children throughout the different ages
and stages of their physical, emotional, and sexual
development.

- *One of the greatest myths, misconceptions, and outright errors
  in thinking about human sexuality is that if we teach children*
  about *sex, they will go out and have sex.* Quite the opposite is true. Scared to open the S-E-X floodgates with
  your children? Don't be! Many parents fear that giving
  information about sexual health equals giving children
  permission to have sex. However, research shows that
  parents who are more open in their discussions about
  sexuality have kids who are *less* likely to become sexually active at a young age. . . . Talk early and talk often.

- *Start with what you can see.* We talk about fallopian tubes,
  sperm, and reproduction before we even teach children about their genitals. It just makes more sense to
  start with what you can see and work your way in as it
  becomes cognitively and developmentally appropriate.
  Think about it this way: we teach our children about
  their ears and earlobes long before we start referencing
  cochlea, Eustachian tubes, and tympanic membranes.
  Why is that? We give them concepts that they can handle
  and grasp as they are ready for them. Sexuality education is no different.

- *When do you start sexuality education at home?* Today! It is
  crucial at every step in a child's development. For more
  information regarding age-appropriate information to
  discuss with children, visit DrDae.com.

❖

"Sex-as-dirty and women-as-tainted messages are central
to the virginity movement," Valenti wrote in *The Purity
Myth*.[33] "Pleasure is widely dismissed, if not denounced, in
the virginity movement. When the purpose of sex is simply
procreation, pleasure is simply gratuitous."[34] And she wrote,
"Abstinence-only education seeks to create a world where
everyone is straight, women are relegated to the home,
the only appropriate family is a nuclear one, reproductive
choices are negated, and the only sex people have is for
procreation."[35]

But if these things are true, I am not part of the virginity movement. If they are true, chastity is not part of
the virginity movement, either—because for people who
practice chastity, sex is for procreation and unity, not just
procreation, and it's supposed to be pleasurable. The best
part of having read Valenti's book is that what makes her
angry makes me angry, too. The difference is that she and
I associate those things with entirely different movements:
she with the movement of people who practice chastity,
and I with a movement of people who don't. Indeed, myths
about purity circulate, even inside her book. But what is the
truth about purity?

What Is Purity?

As a result of my own aversion to purity culture as described
and decried by lots of bloggers, as well as to the perpetua-
tion of the purity myths, I have tended to avoid using the
word "purity" at all in what I write. But authentic purity *is*
a thing—a good thing, according to proponents of chastity.

Detractors of purity culture contend that purity—
according to purity culture—is something we're born with
and that the "loss" of it necessitates irreparable shame and
lifelong guilt. I disagree with this definition of purity, but
when I tried to come up with a better one, I discovered I

actually couldn't. So I made a request of my followers on Facebook and Twitter: define purity.

Some said purity means "stain free, undefiled, without blemish." Another said it means "not spotless, but knowing good, and trying to be good." One called purity "beauty," another called it "holiness," and another called it "innocence." Others still called it "the state in which we are able to love most effectively," or "setting aside your desires for the things of the world," or "putting yourself last." One person called it "virginity," which didn't sound right to me, because it meant anybody who has ever had sex is "impure," including married couples.

As I read all the responses, most of which were unique, purity's definition didn't become clearer to me. Instead, I started to wonder if, as a group, we even really know what it is. So I searched for it in the *Catechism of the Catholic Church*, which says:

> Baptism confers on its recipient the grace of purification from all sins. But the baptized must continue to struggle against concupiscence of the flesh and disordered desires. With God's grace he will prevail . . .

- by the virtue and gift of chastity, for chastity lets us love with upright and undivided hearts;

- by purity of intention which consists in seeking the true end of man: with simplicity of vision, the baptized person seeks to find and to fulfill God's will in everything;

- by purity of vision, external and internal;

- by discipline of feelings and imagination;

- by refusing all complicity in impure thoughts that incline us to turn aside from the path of God's commandments . . . [and]

- by prayer. (CCC 2520)

In other words, God purifies us through Baptism, though we still tend to sin, a tendency kept in check by practicing chastity, by having intentions that don't contradict the Christian life, by having discipline, and by praying. The focus in purity culture is on maintaining a purity we are "born" with, when we're not born with purity at all, nor are we responsible for attaining or maintaining it. What the focus is supposed to be on instead is the person who makes purity possible: Jesus Christ.

Purity isn't about what you are worth. Purity is given to you, regardless of sin, *because* of what you are worth. Purity isn't about not sinning ever (that's impossible for us); it is achieved by the only guy who never sinned. Purity isn't about setting certain sins aside as unforgiveable; it is the reason we can overcome *any* sin. Purity isn't about having a way to judge each other; it is a reason not to judge each other. It isn't about scaring people into living certain kinds of lives; it's a reminder of the mercy we will be given when we don't.

But what do we do when somebody makes it about those things—when somebody uses "purity" to alienate people who haven't practiced chastity? A video of a talk given by Protestant minister Matt Chandler at a 2009 conference answers this question.[36] Matt tells a story about taking a friend to a worship service. His friend—a twenty-six-year-old single mom—had been in a relationship with a married man. Naturally, Matt was horrified when, from the front of the room, a preacher announced that his sermon would be about sex. At the start of the sermon, Matt said,

the preacher held up a red rose and smelled it. Then the
preacher threw the rose into the congregation. "Everybody
needs to smell this," the preacher said. "Touch it." About
a thousand high-school students and young adults passed
the rose from person to person, until the end of the sermon,
when the preacher asked for it back.

"Some kid came up," Matt said in his story, and handed
the "jacked up" rose back to the preacher. Like the cup of
spit water in Sarah Bessey's story, the rose the preacher
held was supposed to represent a person who hasn't saved
sex for marriage. After passing through a thousand sets of
hands, the rose was broken—it wasn't as pretty as it was
when the preacher first held it up. But he held it up again:
"Now who would want *this*?"

That's when Matt shouted in his story what he wished
he had shouted at the preacher: "Jesus wants the rose!"

That, Matt said, is the point of the Gospel.

And he's right. Because of the Gospel, purity isn't your
responsibility. Your job is to follow and believe. Let Jesus
do the rest.

Truth

The Most Important
Part of the Story

"If you see your way clearly, follow it."

—*St. Josemaría Escrivá, in* The Way

In the heat of Florida's version of February, I popped the hood of my aging car, propped it open, and leaned over the engine to check the oil. (Lest you are misled, topping the oil off is one of only three things I can do with cars. I can also pump gas and drive.) Afterward, I walked up the driveway toward the open garage.

This is where I first encountered the bee.

Since childhood, I have had an aversion to all creatures that creep, crawl, or fly—and a particularly irrational aversion when creatures that creep, crawl, or fly are covered in fuzz. The black-and-yellow bee flew past me and into the garage. This is when I noticed the puff of fuzz that covered

it. Already, I harbored disdain for the bee—at a social disadvantage due solely to its anatomy—even though he or
she was in no apparent way interested in me. But I stood
on the line that divides the driveway from the garage and
watched it. The bee, I observed, intended to land on nearly
every item in the garage at least once.

Fudge.

The bee landed on the treadmill first. Then it spent
a couple of seconds on the stationary bike—and then on
the fridge, and then on the bench. Then it flew toward the
clothesline, which was a problem because the part of the
garage in which I do laundry is as far from the outdoors as
the garage gets. It isn't easy to lure a bee back outside from
there. I decided I wouldn't leave my post at the top of the
driveway until the bee left the garage. But quickly, I could
conclude that the bee did not want to leave. It flew from
the clothesline onward to a stack of books, to a Rubbermaid
container, and to a recycling bin, and slowly and surely back
toward the driveway.

Finally, I got brave. I walked past the bee until it was
closer to the exit than I was. Then I turned toward it and
spoke.

"Get. Out."

The bee didn't leave, so I shouted.

"Get out! Get out of my garage!"

No luck. *Fudge!* The bee dillydallied while I wandered
further into the garage, trying to decide what to do next. *This
is my garage. I work out here. I do laundry here. I cannot have
a bee here while I do these things.* I stomped my feet a little. I
may have shaken a fist.

"YOU. GET. OUT."

The bee finally flew toward the line that separates the
garage floor from the driveway. I watched it cross the line,
float over the driveway into the yard, and fly away from my

house until the bee had gotten so far from me I no longer could see it at all. Then I noticed what I hadn't seen throughout the entire bee encounter: my neighbor. And I was pretty sure she had seen everything.

Except for the bee.

The bee, as it turns out, is the most important part of the story. What a person does when he or she encounters a bee (just think of your own experiences) might be cause for concern for people who, from afar, can't see the bee. They have no evidence that what you are doing is an acceptable response to your experience—a response to something real. Some people, of course, *will* assume there is a living, breathing, fuzz-covered reason for what you do. Others will return to their homes with haste and lock their doors.

In our culture, single adults have sex with the people they date. So as a twenty-nine-year-old woman who has never had sex (and may never have sex), who doesn't date guys who won't save sex for marriage, and who is not ashamed to discuss her virginity in very public forums, a lot of people think I'm crazy. But it is akin to when a neighbor is too far from a bee to know it is the reason I do what I do (such as stomp my feet and yell, "Fudge!"). People who are far from chastity don't understand why I don't have sex.

How I live—without sex—has been cause for concern, at least for readers who have felt compelled to admit that to me. What I do, how I date, and that I talk about it so publicly doesn't make sense to them. Like a neighbor too far away to see the bee at which I shout, distant onlookers need the most important part of the story in order for what they have seen to start to make sense.

My life is not inexplicable. What I do—and do not do— is a response to something real.

Getting Ready for the Birds and Bees

As a fourth grader in 1971, Linda dodged potholes as she walked along Alstyne Avenue in Queens, New York. She stopped when she saw a group of girls her age loitering at a car parked parallel to the curb, and she joined them. Over a distant siren and the lively shouts of neighborhood schoolmates at play, Linda listened intently to the conversation. One of the girls said another had gotten her period.

"I didn't understand what that meant," Linda said, which changed the course of the discussion. The other girls told her to ask her mom to explain it. In a panic, Linda ran home and to her room, where her mother found her crying.

"What's the matter?" asked her mom.

"What is a period and why don't I know about it?"

Her mom looked surprised and wanted to know why Linda had asked. Obviously aggravated that somebody had brought it up to Linda, her mother left the room. But she returned a few minutes later, after she had retrieved a box, which she handed to her daughter.

"You should read this," her mother said, "and ask questions if you need to."

"She'd sent away for it from Kotex, or Tampax, or something," said Linda. "A little period start-up kit." Half the package, she said, was the part parents are supposed to read to help them prepare to talk about periods with their children. As a result of the experience, Linda felt entirely on her own.

When Linda was in seventh or eighth grade at St. Leo Catholic School, the nun who taught Linda's religion class required the students to read the textbook's sex chapter and discuss it with a parent. When she told her mother about the assignment, "the color drained from her face," Linda said. "You'd think I'd said, 'OK, now I'm going to remove your gall bladder.'" Her mother was uncomfortable, her answers short, and her aversion to the discussion obvious. Linda's mom did not want to talk about sex.

"It was disappointing," said Linda. So Linda figured out the facts of life on her own, by reading the encyclopedia and hearing things on the street—"literally on the street, in New York," she said.

Linda's experience is not uncommon, and the consequences of experiences like it can be unfortunate. Parents who avoid talking about sex with kids, according to a study published in 2010 by *Perspectives on Sexual and Reproductive Health*, tend to avoid talking about sex because they believe "their children are not ready to hear about it. At the same time, however, parents recognized that their children are regularly exposed to a wide range of negative sexual influences, whether they are ready for it or not."[37]

So before her own children were born, Linda made a decision. "I was going to be open and communicative. I wanted [my kids] to be comfortable with themselves, with their bodies." She planned to provide opportunities for her kids to "get the facts" from her and to receive guidance and direction. She intended to "set the foundation that sex is very important, that it's not a topic that should be ignored," she said.

And she did. I can attest to it, because Linda is my mom.

What Does It Mean to Be "Human"?

I sat at the window seat at the dining-room table, beneath the glow of the brown-glass and brushed-gold chandelier that hung from the white, popcorn ceiling at the house where I grew up. There, my mom told me how babies are made. I was a wide-eyed fourth grader, moderately riveted and mildly disturbed. My mom, who aced every human anatomy class she ever had to take, used a Bic pen to draw a uterus on a napkin.

My brother remembers a formal sex talk, too. "Mom used her anatomy textbooks," he said. He can also recall a series of informal discussions with our dad, in "bits and pieces over the course of fifteen years."

More important than my mom's ability to draw a killer uterus was what her decision to draw it represented: her availability. Thanks to her and my dad, our home was a safe place. We had no taboo topics. My brother and I could ask our parents anything. This didn't mean we asked about everything (nor did it mean our questions never elicited uncomfortable answers). But we knew that if and when we wanted to ask whatever we wanted to ask, we could. The reward for kids in a household like ours is not solely access to good information but the desire to acquire it—a thirst for truth that doesn't end.

It was this thirst for truth that compelled me to learn most of what I know about sex. I discovered that humans are created with the ability to make responsible sexual decisions and that our bodies—which are sexual—are temples. They are dwelling places of God. I learned we can learn self-mastery through the practice of chastity, which promotes the dignity of all human life and the sanctity of sexual activity. I learned, too, that we are created able to maintain sexual fidelity, even in a culture that isn't confident a husband and wife can honor each other for the rest of their lives.

"Strict sexual fidelity is a lofty but perhaps fundamentally doomed aspiration," wrote Meghan Laslocky, author of *The Little Book of Heartbreak: Love Gone Wrong Through the Ages*, in a CNN.com column.[38] According to Laslocky, humans have to tolerate the "impulse to experience sexual variety" even more now than in previous generations, because people are living longer now than before. "A person is theoretically expected to have one sexual partner for about fifty years," she wrote. "This seems like a lot to expect of any human being—even the most honorable, ethical, and moral." It's a lot to expect, she said, because humans are animals and animals aren't often monogamous. To Laslocky, infidelity is "only human," and monogamy is "unnatural."

While her viewpoint is rarely contested in popular culture, it's so very incorrect. As I discovered in my quest for truth, infidelity is *not* "only human." *Fidelity* is. Humans are embodied spirits, created in God's image, given enough daily grace to resist temptation. "Original sin," according to the *Catechism*, "caused a deprivation of original holiness and justice, but human nature has not been totally corrupted; it is wounded . . . and inclined to sin—an inclination to evil that is called concupiscence" (CCC 405).

Concupiscence is in "the impulse to experience sexual variety." It is what interests a married man or woman in having sex with somebody other than his or her spouse. But we have to learn to master our impulses. It is animal to act thoughtlessly on an impulse but it is human to use faith and reason to control it. It is animal to be unfaithful but it is human to keep our vows. This doesn't mean we are animals because we sin. It does mean we are *fallen* and in need of divine grace.

We don't sin because we're human; we sin because, for a moment, we forget what it means to be human. Humans aren't bound by self-centered impulses but are free to rise above them. We don't have to keep making the same mistakes over and over again. If we become the animals Laslocky says we are, it isn't because of biology. It's because we abdicated our freedom to choose that which is most human, to choose the good and true and beautiful.

In *Veritatis Splendor*, St. John Paul II reminds us: "If redeemed man still sins, this is not due to an imperfection

of Christ's redemptive act, but to man's will not to avail
himself of the grace which flows from that act. God's com-
mand is of course proportioned to man's capabilities; but
to the capabilities of the man to whom the Holy Spirit has
been given" (*Veritatis Splendor* 103).

The Grace of Saved Sex

Because of this grace, I am not saving myself for marriage.
    That isn't a typo.
    I am not saving *myself* for marriage. We can't save our-
selves—only Christ can save us. What I am saving . . . is sex.
The "save" in "saving sex" is not the same as the "save" in
"saving the sandwich for later." If I get married, I will have
waited to have sex, yes. But when I say I am "*saving* sex," I
don't mean I'm "putting it off."
    When I say I am "saving sex," I mean I'm redeeming
it. By God's grace, I have chosen to resist the damaging cultural trends that trivialize the purpose of human sexuality.
I refuse to use or regard the human body in any way that
doesn't revere its dignity or its sanctity. In marriage, sex is
a gift of the totality of oneself to another person. (It's not
the only way spouses give themselves to one another, but
it is an affirmation of the vows they made on their wedding
day.) Waiting for sex until marriage protects parts of me: the
physical, emotional, and spiritual. But if I focus too hard on
how saving sex protects me, an important truth is neglected:
saving sex protects *sex*.
    Sex in our culture is more about getting than giving.
The world says part of sex is important (pleasure). While
that part of it *is* important, all the other parts of it are important, too. Our culture, however, says parts of it aren't necessary (such as fertility and unity beyond the biological). Our
culture says that we who wait are wrong to wait because

"everybody's doing it," because in our culture, says Dr. Peter Kreeft, "Consensus determines rightness or wrongness."[39]

A lot of people say you have to know you'll like sex with somebody before you marry him or her. A lot of people say marriage is just a "sheet of paper," that sex isn't sacred, because if it were, people wouldn't have multiple partners. But what if how true these things are isn't actually determined by "a lot of people"? Maybe marriage is only a sheet of paper when you treat it as if it's a sheet a paper. Maybe sex is only not sacred when you treat it as if it isn't. This is why you could say the people who wait until they are married to have sex, and the people who would like to have sex but are celibate because of what they believe about sex, and even the priests and nuns who keep their chastity vows all have this in common: we are saving sex—redeeming it—by treating it like it's sacred.

What Is Love?

There is a viral YouTube video called "What Is Love?" in which an elderly man says he doesn't "count it a burden" to care for his wife, who has Alzheimer's disease. In segments on screen, he helps her into her wheelchair, into the car, and onto the custom bike chair on the front of the bicycle he rides when he takes her to the beach. "From the moment she gets up to the moment she goes to bed, I do absolutely everything," he said. "[I] clean her teeth, shower, dress, everything, but . . . I count it a great privilege to care for this woman I've loved all of these years, and continue to love."

Another viral video, called "Danny and Annie," is an animation of interviews with a real-life couple, conducted as Danny nears his death. Throughout their marriage, Danny wrote a love letter for Annie every day. "I could write on and on about her," Danny said. "She lights up the room in the morning when she tells me to put both hands on her shoulders so she can support me. She lights up my life when she says to me at night, 'Wouldn't you like a little ice cream?' or, 'Would you please drink more water?' I mean, those aren't very romantic things to say, but they stir my heart."

Both couples' stories are reminders of what most people don't think about when an usher opens the narthex doors, revealing the bride so she can meet her groom at the altar. We don't routinely think about disease or death at weddings, because it's morbid and we don't want to—and that's OK. We don't have to be people who dwell on all the bad things that could happen during a marriage: illness or injury, natural disaster, loss of a child, unemployment, bankruptcy, unexpected relocation, addiction, a house fire, family conflict, a disparity in household responsibilities, a sick toddler, a stolen vehicle, or a baby who takes off her own poopy diaper and uses it to paint the wall beside her crib (sorry, Mom). The point is to become people who can keep vows even when bad things happen.

People "suffer," wrote John Janaro, author of *Never Give Up: My Life and God's Mercy* and associate professor emeritus of theology at Christendom College.[40] "It's important to marry someone who will suffer with you and with whom you are willing to suffer. There's nothing 'romantic' about the daily, ordinary, often banal suffering that you will have to share. But it's there that your love grows as trust, commitment, and fidelity."

Premarital sex doesn't prepare us for this. Sex is good practice for sex; patience is good practice for marriage. Chastity helps us cultivate other skills that are readily transferable to marriage: governing our urges, creating and maintaining healthy boundaries, respecting somebody else's boundaries, accepting discomfort, communicating, making sacrifices, having empathy, and making selfless decisions. By not having sex when we date, we build these skills. Our future marriages are potentially enriched by these skills. A marriage is not intrinsically impaired if a newlywed couple's sexual relationship has to start with awkward practice, direct conversation, and a sense of humor. Chastity prepares us for that, and it teaches us to trust.

The Gift of Generous Living

On a weekday morning, I slowed my car to a stop before I made a right on red next to an elderly homeless woman. Her sign—"Homeless. Anything Appreciated."—etched in Sharpie on a scrap of cardboard caught my attention and hurt my heart. Despite the desire to stop to help, I decided aloud in my car that I wouldn't.

"Nope," I said. "I have nothing to give her." But as soon as I completed my turn, I pulled my car off the road and onto the shoulder.

"What am I *doing*?" I'll tell you what I was doing: exactly what I didn't want to do. I checked my rearview mirror for the woman. She still stood at the corner, behind my car now, and almost certainly had seen me pull off the street. I had too soft a heart and too big an ego not to search for something to give since I already had stopped. I discovered a reservoir of loose change in my console and dug through it for quarters so the good stuff would dominate the handful of money I would give. I got out of the car, awkwardly walked the bumpy dirt path that led to her, and held up my hands, full of change.

"This is for you," I said.

Her eyes, wide and watery, met mine as she held open her bag, into which I poured the money. She thanked me sincerely, and said, "God bless you." I walked back to the car, sat in my seat, and merged onto the street.

Once my workday was underway, I forgot about the encounter. At lunchtime, I walked to Café Eden—an eatery

at the back of a health-food store near my office—where I
was a regular. I ordered my meal, and when the chef slid
my plate of food toward me, I slid a wad of cash across the
counter toward him. But he pushed it back.

"What are you doing?" I picked up the cash and held
it up at him.

"No," he said. "Keep it. Today, lunch is on us."

Baffled but grateful, I picked up my plate and picked
out a table. While I ate, the image of the homeless woman
returned for the first time that day, and for the first time
in adulthood, I understood what it means to trust Christ.
In pulling my car off the road and offering the homeless
woman what I had, I had chosen generosity where I hadn't
before: with my money and my attention. I had never done
anything like it. And while I sat at Café Eden, eating a free
lunch, I finally believed we *can* be generous—that we can
give what we have to people who need it more and trust
that we still will be taken care of. For lots of people, "to
give" something implies "to lose" something. But Jesus, who
instructs us not to worry, promises otherwise: "Look at the
birds of the air, that they do not sow, nor reap nor gather
into barns, and yet your heavenly Father feeds them. Are
you not worth much more than they?"(Mt. 6:26).

For once, I hadn't hoarded what I had. I gave it away.
And in the end, at the café, I still got what I needed. That
day I learned that when I trust Jesus, I am better equipped to
do what he asks me to do. He is the ultimate unconditional
lover, the God who provides, who teaches us how to live.
Chastity would not be possible for me if I didn't believe this.
I, like some respondents to some of my informal surveys,
would worry too much that wedding night sex would disap-
point me or that newlywed sex would expose an enduring
incompatibility.

But why do we worry?

I profess a faith that requires me to trust that God arranged for a virgin to give birth. Why do I think my husband and I can't get something very good out of figuring sex out together, within the safety of the sacrament of Matrimony? I indeed won't know what I am doing or what to expect on my wedding night. But I've said it before and I'll say it again and again: In not knowing what we're doing, we express confidence in a spouse's commitment. In not knowing what to expect, we infuse our vows with authenticity.

And in the process, we exemplify a truth I have embraced: Chastity *Is* for lovers.

Acknowledgments

To write a book has been a dream since I was in about second grade, when reading books monopolized my time. I am grateful to all of the people who helped me make it happen, especially:

The person—whoever you are—who sent Patrick the link to my blog, for doing so.

Patrick McGowan, for taking a chance on a "green" girl who had a growing platform and a big dream, for reading my proposal before I turned it in for real, and for believing what I could write was worth a publisher's time.

Heidi Saxton—this book's editor—for the letter you wrote when you read the first set of chapters I showed you, for ideas and direction, and for putting up with my semifrequent, sleep-deprivation-induced "I have no idea what I am doing" e-mails.

Jon O'Neill and Samantha Fuchs, for being editors for me before I had one.

Any editor I have ever worked with at the *Tampa Bay Times*, including Mike Konrad, for giving a high-school senior a shot; Jon O'Neill, for confidence in my work; Marlene Sokol, for hiring me; Molly Moorhead, for hiring me the second time; Bridget Grumet, for periodically dedicating space in the *Pasco Times* to my opinion; and Jim Verhulst, for saying yes when I asked to write about sex for your section.

My undergrad and grad school professors,—especially Rick Wilber, Gil Thelen, Richard Aregood, Liisa Hyvarinen-Temple, Randy Miller, Larry Leslie, Kristin Arnold, Richard Downing, Ryan Henry, Gary Dudell,

Tennyson Wright, and Dae Sheridan—for teaching me what I know and expressing faith in my ability to apply it.

The people who read my blog and follow me on Twitter, Facebook, and Google+; and Our Lady of Hope, St. Francis de Sales, and St. John Paul II, all for praying with me and for me while I wrote.

My friends, for still being my friends after I stopped socializing to write a book, and for believing I could do it.

My whole family, for cheering me on.

My brother, for listening the time I called you crying because I was sure I would fail at writing a book (and for not agreeing with me).

And my parents, for everything, but particularly for letting me spread my notes, books, and bowls of pretzels across multiple rooms in your house while writing; for participating in dance breaks between chapters; for exemplifying common sense, critical thought, and hard work; for raising me exactly the way you did; for always providing an environment in which I could ask questions, and for not ever being afraid to answer them.

Discussion Questions

Chapter 1. Chastity: A Better Sexual Ethic

1. Chastity isn't restrictive like shackles are restrictive. It's restrictive like boundaries, which keep what could hurt us out of our space. What good boundaries does (or could) chastity create for you?

2. People don't resent chastity because it's bad to be chaste. They resent it because it's hard to be chaste. But "hard" does not negate "good." What about chastity is most difficult for you? Why is that part of chastity good for you, despite how hard it is?

3. When we determine how good something is by how moderately we can use it (i.e., "everything in moderation"), we avert an important discernment process: *do I actually need it in my life?* Make a list of the pursuits that take up most of your time outside work or school. Do you need each pursuit in your life? What do you need more of in your life that didn't make the list?

Chapter 2. Virginity: Easier Done Than Said

1. Virgins are largely portrayed by the media as socially awkward. So it is difficult for many people to imagine that some people are sexually inexperienced by choice. In what ways might the world be different if the people in it were not averse to virginity?

2. In what ways do we perceive sex differently because of what we see on TV?

3. According to one school of thought, we should eliminate the word "virginity" from the vernacular because of its polarizing effect within the Christian community: It's associated with pressuring young people into keeping it and shaming those who don't. How can we encourage premarital virginity without using fear or shame?

Chapter 3. Providence: A Reason for Reckless Abandon

1. Sometimes God's silence *is* his provision. In what ways has God blessed you or spared you suffering by *not* giving you what you wanted?

2. If you don't yet know what your vocation is, what are you doing now to discern it? What could you do that you haven't done yet? If you already know your vocation, what are you doing now to live it out? What parts of your living it out could use improvement?

3. Feeling sorry for yourself when you're unhappy about things that aren't within your control doesn't make you happy. Changing your perspective does. What, if anything, makes you unhappy lately? What new perspectives of it could you adopt?

Chapter 4. Dating: A Road to Marriage

1. Consider past pursuits of relationships that didn't work out as you'd hoped. Given that a dating relationship is "successful" if through it you discover the truth about the person you date, were any of these past pursuits successful? In what ways has discovering the truth about the people you used to date helped determine how (or whom) you date now?

2. We all date for different reasons. In previous relationships, what factors resulted in your decision to agree

to date someone? What factors might you consider instead next time you discern a dating relationship with someone?

3. Is it a good idea for a person who is chaste to date somebody who isn't? Why or why not? What should a person do who discovers that the person he or she is dating does not want to practice chastity?

Chapter 5. Love: The Hardest Thing You'll Ever Have to Do

1. Why is it important to differentiate between being in love with someone and truly loving someone? How do you know whether you are *in* love with somebody, or if you *love* him or her?

2. Some of us have been and some of us will be broadsided by our significant others' essentially profane declarations: "I don't love you anymore." Why, in our culture, do people stop loving the people to whom they once were committed? Is it possible to choose to love a person while we don't feel "in love" with him or her? Why or why not?

3. All of us are called to love. Regardless of your relationship status, how can you fulfill your vocation to love today?

Chapter 6. Self-Control: A Response to the Contraception Controversy

1. The Catholic Church opposes the use of contraception because it negates half of what the Church says is the purpose of sex. Do you share the Church's position? Why or why not?

2. During several widely publicized contraception controversies, people who disagree with the Church implied that the Church does not promote sexual health. In what

ways is that implication false? In what ways *does* the Church promote sexual health?

3. Contraception is favored in our culture because of what it prevents. But it is not lack of access to contraception that transmits disease or causes unplanned pregnancy; having sex transmits disease and causes unplanned pregnancy. What are some of the underlying cultural assumptions that need to be challenged to drive home the truth about this?

Chapter 7. Purity: Not Your Responsibility

1. Youth pastors sometimes use analogies to encourage youth to save sex for marriage (e.g., not saving sex is like giving your spouse old shoes, or used gum, or cookies covered in dirt as a gift). Were you exposed to analogies such as these while you grew up? In what ways are they (or are they not) effective? If you were going to encourage a group of teenagers to save sex for marriage, how would you do it?

2. Do you find yourself averse to what many in the Christian blogosphere decry as "purity culture"? Why or why not?

3. Despite efforts in youth ministry to encourage premarital abstinence while kids are growing up, the majority grow into adults who have premarital sex. Is it still important to encourage premarital abstinence? How can youth ministers do that better?

Chapter 8. Truth: The Most Important Part of the Story

1. My decision not to have sex as long as I'm not married is incomprehensible to some people. Have you ever been misunderstood for sticking to your convictions? Why were those beliefs and values so important to you? Is it always necessary to argue until you change someone else's

mind? How do you know when it's time to walk away from the argument?

2. How, if at all, did your parents discuss sex with you while you grew up? What *didn't* your parents teach you that you would teach your own kids? What is implied about sex by a parent who never discusses it with their kids? Why does a kid need an introduction to sex from his or her parents?

3. Trust is hard, but trust is worth it. With what areas of your life would you like to trust God more than you do? What can you do today to express that trust?

Notes

1. Anjani Chandra, William D. Mosher, and Casey Copen, "Sexual Behavior, Sexual Attraction, and Sexual Identity in the United States: Data From the 2006–2008 National Survey of Family Growth, Centers for Disease Control and Prevention" (March 2011), accessed 2013, http://www.cdc.gov/nchs/data/nhsr/nhsr036.pdf.

2. Tyler Charles, "(Almost) Everyone's Doing It," *Relevant Magazine* (September 2011), accessed 2013, http://www.relevantmagazine.com/life/relationships/almost-everyones-doing-it.

3. Christina Pesoli, "How Abstinence-Only Messages Steer Girls Wrong," *Huffington Post*, May 22, 2013, accessed 2013, http://www.huffingtonpost.com/christina-pesoli/how-abstinence-only-messages-steer-girls-wrong_b_3321069.html.

4. Karol Wojtyla, *Love and Responsiblity* (San Francisco: Ignatius Press, 1993), 143.

5. John Blake, "Why Young Christians Aren't Waiting Anymore," CNN.com, Sept. 27, 2011, accessed 2013, http://religion.blogs.cnn.com/2011/09/27/why-young-christians-arent-waiting-anymore/.

6. Chandra, Mosher, Copen, "Sexual Behavior, Sexual Attraction, and Sexual Identity in the United States."

7. Jessica C. Henriquez,"My Virginity Mistake," Salon.com, May 5, 2013, accessed 2013, http://www.salon.com/2013/05/06/my_virginity_mistake/.

8. Emily Maynard, "The Day I Turned In My V-Card," *Prodigal Magazine*, accessed 2013, http://www.prodigalmagazine.com/the-day-i-turned-in-my-v-card/.

9. Abigail Rine, "Why Some Evangelicals Are Trying to Stop Obsessing Over Pre-Marital Sex," *Atlantic*, May 23, 2013, accessed 2013, http://www.theatlantic.com/sexes/archive/2013/05/why-some-evangelicals-are-trying-to-stop-obsessing-over-pre-marital-sex/276185/.

10. Jason DeParle and Sabrina Tavernise, "For Women under 30, Most Births Occur Outside Marriage," *New York Times*, February 17, 2012, accessed 2013, http://www.nytimes.com/2012/02/18/us/for-women-under-30-most-births-occur-outside-marriage.html?pagewanted=all&_r=0.

11. Edward Sri, *Men, Women and the Mystery of Love: Practical Insights from John Paul II's* Love and Responsibility (Cincinnati, OH: Servant Books, 2007), 14.

12. Elna Baker, "Yes, I'm a 27-Year-Old Virgin," *Glamour*, September 11, 2009, accessed 2013, http://www.glamour.com/sex-love-life/2009/09/yes-im-a-27-year-old-virgin.

13. Ibid.

14. Ibid.

15. Sri, *Men, Women and the Mystery of Love*, 12–14.

16. Wojtyla, *Love and Responsiblity*, 123.

17. Sri, *Men, Women and the Mystery of Love*, 56.

18. Ibid., 79.

19. Ibid., 59.

20. Ibid., 79–80.

21. Wojtyla, *Love and Responsiblity*, 234.

22. Ibid., 228, 230.

23. For more information on natural family planning, see http://www.usccb.org/issues-and-action/marriage-and-family/natural-family-planning/what-is-nfp/.

24. Sri, *Men, Women and the Mystery of Love*, 55.

25. Sarah Bessey, "I Am Damaged Goods," *A Deeper Story*, January 29, 2013, accessed 2014, http://deeperstory.com/i-am-damaged-goods/.

26. Preston Yancey, "When Purity Culture Hurts Men, Too," *Preston Yancey*, February 5, 2013, accessed January 18, 2014, http://prestonyancey.com/blog/2013/02/when-purity-culture-hurts-men-too.

27. Anne Almasy, "The Vulgar Face of Purity Culture," *Huffington Post*, September 16, 2013, accessed January 19, 2014, http://

www.huffingtonpost.com/anne-almasy/the-vulgar-face-of-purity_b_3882864.html.

28. Jonalyn Grace Fincher, "Breaking Shame: Why Purity Culture Works," *Ruby Slippers*, May 15, 2013, accessed January 19, 2014, http://soulation.org/jonalynblog/2013/05/fighting-shame-why-purity-culture-works.html.

29. Kendall Davis, "The Twisted Lies of Purity Culture," *Convergent Books*, August 30, 2013, accessed January 19, 2014, http://www.convergentbooks.com/purity-culture-and-a-fear-of-boys/.

30. Jessica Valenti, *The Purity Myth: How America's Obsession with Virginity Is Hurting Young Women* (Berkeley: Seal Press, 2010), 49.

31. Ibid., 91.

32. Ibid., 92.

33. Ibid., 33.

34. Ibid., 43.

35. Ibid., 111.

36. "Matt Chandler—Jesus Wants the Rose," YouTube, December 21, 2010, accessed January 17, 2014, http://www.youtube.com/watch?v=5iY_tmektJc.

37. Ellen K. Wilson, Barbara T. Dalberth, Helen P. Koo, and Jennifer C. Gard, "Parents' Perspectives on Talking to Preteenage Children about Sex," *Perspectives on Sexual and Reproductive Health* 42 (2010): 56–63., accessed January 2014, doi:10.1363/4205610.

38. Meghan Laslocky, "Face It: Monogamy Is Unnatural," CNN Opinion, June 21, 2013, accessed 2013, http://www.cnn.com/2013/06/21/opinion/laslocky-monogamy-marriage/.

39. Peter Kreeft, *Back to Virtue*, (San Francisco: Ignatius Press, 1992), 26.

40. John Janaro, "A Meditation on Marriage Vows," *Arleen Spenceley*, December 16, 2013, accessed 2014, http://www.arleenspenceley.com/2013/12/guest-post-john-janaro-meditation-on.html.

Arleen Spenceley graduated from the University of South Florida in 2007 with a bachelor of arts degree in journalism and in 2013 with a master of arts degree in rehabilitation and mental health counseling. She first wrote professionally in high school as a correspondent for the *Tampa Bay Times* and joined the *Times* as a staff writer during college. Her work has also appeared in the *Chicago Sun-Times*, the *Austin-American Statesman*, the *Journal Gazette*, and the *Herald Times* in Indiana; the *Norristown Times Herald*, the *Star-Courier*, the *Hometown Punxsutawney Magazine*, and the *Dispatch* in Pennsylvania; the *Record Courier* in Ohio; the *Houma Today* and the *Daily Comet* in Louisiana; and the *State* in South Carolina. She has written on a freelance basis since college, including contributions to *Chastity Project* and a monthly column on Ignitum Today. She is a regular contributor to *CatholicMatch. com* and has contributed popular essays to *Relevantmagazine. com*, including "Confessions of a Catholic Christian," and "Is There Room for Erotica in Christianity?" She has also written for *Busted Halo, Relate Magazine,* and *Life Teen.*

Spenceley blogs at arleenspenceley.com about love, relationships, and sex, and about the impact of American culture on Christianity from a Roman Catholic perspective. In January 2013, she participated in a roundtable discussion of abstinence and virginity on NPR's nationally syndicated radio show *Tell Me More.* Though she left the *Tampa Bay Times* in 2012 to finish her master's degree, she returned to the *Times* staff in October 2013.